PAINTED
WOODEN
FURNITURE

PAINTED WOODEN FURNITURE

Easy-to-follow templates for decorating over 20 stylish projects

Cate Withacy

krause publications

A QUARTO BOOK

Copyright © 1997 Quarto Inc.

ISBN 0-87341-539-6

 **krause publications**

700 E. State Street, Iola, WI 54990-0001
Telephone: 715/445-2214

Please call or write for our free catalog of publications. Our toll-free
number to place an order or obtain a free catalog is 800-258-0929 or
please use our regular business telephone 715-445-2214 for editorial
comment and further information.

This book was designed and produced by
Quarto Publishing plc
The Old Brewery
6 Blundell Street
London N7 9BH

Senior art editors Antonio Toma, Julie Francis
Designer Peter Laws
Editors Cathy Marriott, Ann Baggaley
Text editor Mary Green
Managing editor Sally MacEachern
Photographers David Sherwin, Martin Norris
Illustrator Sébastien Bertrand
Picture researcher Zoe Holtermann
Art director Moira Clinch
Editorial director Pippa Rubinstein

Typeset in Great Britain by Central Southern Typesetters, Eastbourne
Manufactured in Singapore by Pica Colour Separation Overseas Pte Ltd
Printed in Singapore by Star Standard Industries (Pte) Ltd

CONTENTS

INTRODUCTION

The popularity of painted wooden furniture has endured down the centuries because of the infinite number of ways in which it brightens and enhances our everyday surroundings. The color and vitality of paint combined with the three-dimensional forms of wood create an endless variety of patterns and themes to suit every type of interior and the decorative tastes of every era. No small part of the appeal of painted furniture is that, as a practical craft, it offers opportunities for artistic expression that can be enjoyed by anyone.

Now a truly international craft, painted furniture owes its evolution throughout the world, like any other aspect of civilization, to the impulses of fashion, politics and wealth. The ancient Egyptians' skill in painting on wood, seen in the impressive objects discovered in their tombs, was well appreciated by Europeans, but it was increased contact with the Far East in the eighteenth century that inspired a

passion for painted furniture in Europe, where the influences of the Oriental style on decorative art spread far and wide. As royal patrons commissioned extravagantly ornamented furniture and interiors, the best artisans traveled from court to court, adorning palaces and engaging in an active exchange of ideas and techniques.

While there were talented painters busy decorating the chambers of princes, everyday craftsmen were developing their own tradition. This parallel movement was equally vibrant and, in many cases, just as refined and extremely sophisticated. Especially in the mountainous regions of Central Europe, and in Scandinavia, where long winters spent indoors gave ample opportunity for the perfecting of the craft, painted furniture played a prominent part in the development of regional folk art.

In America, painted furniture achieved as much popularity as it did in Europe, developing a look, style and interpretation all its own, and becoming as varied as that anywhere else in the world. This variety was principally due to the myriad cultural and artistic influences brought to America by groups of European settlers. The most exciting examples of New World joinery were

wooden chests and, later, chairs, tables and cupboards finished with painted decoration.

Painted wooden furniture has adorned dwellings from the most humble to the most sophisticated, and is everywhere appreciated for its vibrancy, its versatility, its character and its warmth. Among decorators, auctioneers and private collectors, it has rapidly become one of the most desirable fields of antique collecting. Today, interest in the craft continues to be renewed, and although contemporary designers no longer adhere to the eighteenth-century concept of co-ordinating room and furniture designs, individual pieces of painted furniture still have relevance to any modern interior. What we have inherited from this grand tradition, with its ancient origins and its constant revitalization, is a treasury of inspiration and an encouragement to take this wonderful art into the next century.

HOW TO USE THIS BOOK

There are 20 original painted furniture projects in this book, involving a variety of techniques. Each is explained in simple stages with illustrated, step-by-step instructions. All the designs can be copied, and enlarged or reduced to fit a chosen area, using the grid provided at the beginning of each project and the photo templates showing the separate elements of each design. Suggestions are given for adapting the patterns to suit alternative pieces of furniture, and the motif library on pages 122 to 125 provides pattern details in easy-to-follow outlines for tracing or drawing.

Photo templates show close-up details of design features

Step-by-step photographs and instructions clearly show the techniques used for each stage of the project

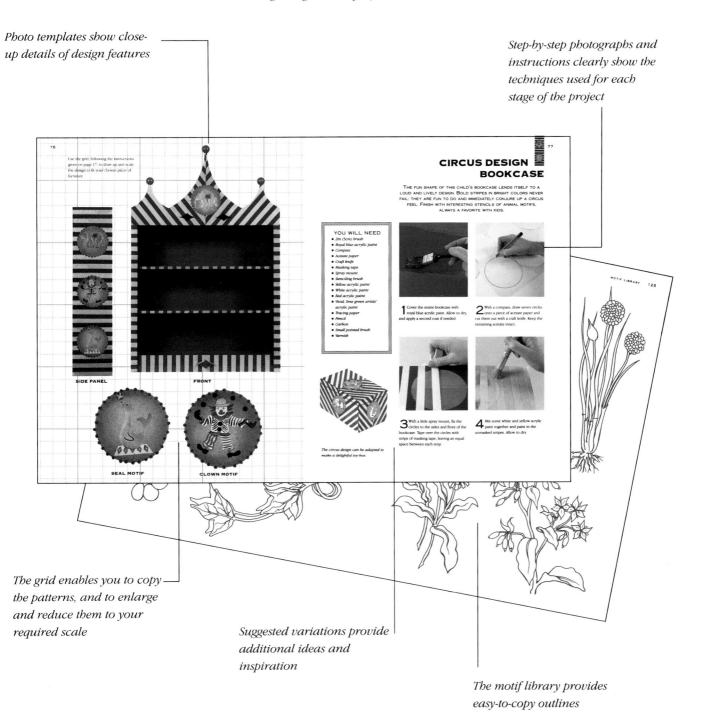

The grid enables you to copy the patterns, and to enlarge and reduce them to your required scale

Suggested variations provide additional ideas and inspiration

The motif library provides easy-to-copy outlines

TOOLS AND MATERIALS

THE BASIC MATERIALS AND EQUIPMENT NEEDED TO COMPLETE THE PROJECTS FEATURED IN THIS BOOK ARE DETAILED BELOW. ALL ARE READILY AVAILABLE EITHER FROM ART MATERIALS SUPPLIERS OR PAINT STORES.

PAINTS

ACRYLIC LATEX: For general purpose decorating, water-based paints come in four basic finishes: flat (matt), satin, semi-gloss and high gloss (enamel). The flat has a dead flat finish when dry and remains absorbent to further coats of paint; always use a flat finish for crackle glazing. The satin finish has a low sheen. It is not absorbent when dry and is therefore water-resistant and washable. Some manufacturers offer an eggshell finish, which looks flat head-on but when viewed at an angle, has a light sheen. Semi-gloss has a higher sheen than satin or eggshell and is somewhat more durable; it's ideal where frequent washing is required. High gloss or enamel is intended as an alternative to oil-based paint. It's designed for use in high-traffic areas that need frequent washing or on items that will be subject to a lot of wear and tear.

ARTISTS' ACRYLICS: Artists' acrylics are available from art materials suppliers. They are more expensive than the decorating water-based paints, but are worth using for motif and detail work and for certain rich strong pigments.

TINTS

ARTISTS' ACRYLICS can also be used as tints for mixing with varnishes and glazes. There are also special *acrylic tints* designed for glaze work and wood graining.

UNIVERSAL TINTING COLORS are available from some paint stores and home centers. Sold in tubes, these are inexpensive and can be mixed with both water- and oil-based products.

SOLVENTS

MINERAL SPIRITS: This is the solvent for all oil-based products. Used to thin oil-based paints and varnishes and to clean any tools used.

DENATURED ALCOHOL: This is a solvent and thinner for French enamel products such as colored enamel varnishes for stained glass painting and shellacs used for French polishing.

WASHING UP LIQUID/DETERGENT: Household detergent can be used with

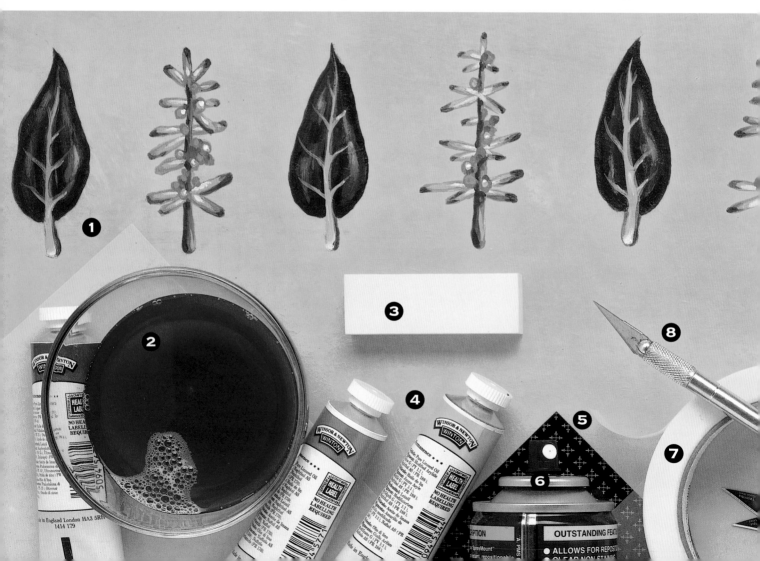

acrylic glazes the way mineral spirits is used with oil-based glaze. The detergent will shift drying glaze which has gone wrong and can be dropped onto a glaze to eat into the glaze where desired.

TAPES

MASKING TAPE is the most commonly used tape to mask out areas when applying paint to other areas of your design. Always rub the edges well into the surface to avoid having the paint bleed in under the masked area, and paint away from the edge of the tape and not into it, to prevent any smudging or bleeding.

LOW TACK TAPE is also available and is useful for complex designs which require a lot of quick masking and remasking.

SPRAY MOUNT is used in graphics projects. It is an excellent light spray glue for fixing tracings and stencils in place while painting or drawing in your design.

PAPERS

TRACING PAPER is a transparent paper which allows the artist to see through to an underlying design. By drawing the design onto the tracing paper the image can be reproduced and reversed if desired.

SANDPAPER: There are different grades of sandpaper, from very coarse, which is ideal for keying old thick layers of paint or varnish, to very fine, suitable for finishing touches to subtle distressing.

STENCILING PAPER AND ACETATE

PAPER: Stenciling paper is a tough, water-resistant card. It is easy to cut with a small, sharp blade or craft knife and stays firm after repeated use due to its waxy coating. *Acetate paper* is also used for stenciling but is transparent and therefore useful for lining up intricate repeat motifs.

CARBON PAPER: This can be used under tracing paper to give a carbon copy of the traced design.

1 *Stenciling paper.*
2 *Household detergent.*
3 *Eraser.*
4 *Artists' acrylics.*
5 *Carbon paper.*
6 *Spray mount.*
7 *Low tack tape.*
8 *Sharp blade for stencil cutting.*
9 *Tracing paper.*
10 *Mineral spirits.*
11 *Acetate paper.*
12 *Measuring tape.*
13 *Sandpaper.*
14 *Masking tape.*
15 *Compass for marking out designs.*

BRUSHES

Basic **DECORATING BRUSHES** are available in a range of sizes, from half inch (1.25cm) up to 5 inch (12.5cm). It is advisable not to go for the cheapest range, as they will often be prone to molting. Always check for loose hairs before applying paint. **ARTISTS' BRUSHES** are ideal for painting furniture. If possible, have on hand a range of smaller brushes for motif detail and lining, a range of pointed brushes to obtain good points and fluid lines in the design detail, and a range of flat-headed fitches for detailed lines and borders and any straight edges. **STENCILING BRUSHES** also vary in size, depending on the nature of the stenciled motif.

They are designed to pounce a little drying paint into the stenciled shape. A **DRAGGING BRUSH** is used for dragging paint or glaze and is therefore flat and firm to give a good lined texture. Hold as parallel to the surface as possible for most control.

SOFTENING BRUSHES can include any very soft and full-haired brush, but a badger hair brush is the ultimate softening brush used by traditional marble painters and wood grainers.

DUSTING BRUSHES are useful for dusting away any fine powder or metal leaf from delicate work which would be ruined by anything harsher.

WOOD GRAINERS OR ROCKERS are the quickest way of achieving a realistic

wood grain, although they do take a bit of mastering. The trick is to use very little glaze and to pull the tool towards you and rock it (hence the name) in one smooth movement.

VARNISHES

Varnishes are available in three finishes: matt, semi-gloss (satin) and gloss. They are also oil-based or water-based. Varnishes will protect artwork and even out the finish on the surface, disguising any dull or shiny patches which may have occurred. They also give an opportunity to change the finish; for example, a piece painted in matt paints can be given a gloss or semi-gloss coating on completion of the artwork.

GLASS PAINTS

These can be oil-based (mineral spirits is the solvent and thinners) or there are denatured alcohol based paints which are colored French enamels (shellacs). Also available are relief liners which imitate the leading in stained glass and can be used to create relief designs.

GILDING MATERIALS

METAL LEAF: This is a cheaper version of real gold leaf, used for traditional oil and water gilding. Metal leaf is available in various golds, copper and silver (aluminum).

GOLD SIZE: This can be oil- or water-based. It acts like a glue developed for applying the metal leaf.

ANTIQUING FLUID

This is an antiquing product designed to put a wash-type layer of umber on a finished piece. The warm umber color gives the artwork an aged look.

GLAZES

Traditionally oil-based, glazes were a mixture of beeswax, linseed oil, and pure turpentine mixed with artists' oil color to produce the glaze used for traditional crafts such as marbling and wood graining. Glazes are now also available in an acrylic (water-based) form and do the same job when mixed with artists' acrylics or acrylic tints.

1 *Acrylic glaze.*
2 *Shellac.*
3 *Varnish.*
4 *Gilding cream for a metallic finish.*
5 *Small pointed artist's brush.*
6 *Fitch.*
7 *Acrylic gold size.*
8 *Glass paint.*
9 *Metal leaf.*
10 *Softening brush.*
11 *Decorating brushes.*
12 *Stenciling brushes.*
13 *Wood grainer or rocker.*
14 *Soft muslin cloth.*
15 *Natural sponge.*
16 *Decorator's sponge.*

FROM PREPARATION TO FINISHING TOUCHES: TECHNICAL TIPS

THE PROJECTS IN THIS BOOK HAVE, AS FAR AS POSSIBLE, BEEN EXECUTED USING ACRYLIC, WATER-BASED PRODUCTS BECAUSE THEY DRY FASTER AND DO NOT REQUIRE ENVIRONMENTALLY UNFRIENDLY THINNERS AND SOLVENTS.

WHAT TO DO BEFORE YOU START YOUR DECORATIVE WORK

Before starting any decorative work on a piece of furniture, some preparation will be necessary whether the item has been worked on before or not.

DEALING WITH EXISTING PAINT

If there is any paint on the piece it will be important to determine what type of paint it is. If it is an oil-based paint and the new decoration is to be water-based acrylic, it will be very important to break up the hard, impermeable surface of the oil-based paints and to give the surface a key; that is, a surface that the acrylic paint can adhere to. Total stripping of the oil-based paint will not always be necessary, unless there are so many old layers of paint that the piece has lost some of its molding detail. In most cases some thorough sanding will be sufficient. If the decorative work is to be achieved with more oil-based paints, then existing layers of oil- or water-based paints will not be a problem; neither will application of acrylics on existing acrylic surfaces. In other words, oil paint will adhere to oil- or water-based existing coats, but acrylic will only adhere to existing acrylic.

To determine which type of paint has been used on an old, second hand piece, paint a small area with an acrylic paint and leave to dry. If when dry the acrylic paint is easy to scrape or peel off, then the existing paint is an oil-based finish. If, however, the acrylic paint adheres well and can only be removed by sanding then the existing paint will likely be a water-based paint.

Before commencing decorative work, smooth away any rough edges with sandpaper.

Use a chisel or nails to "age" a wooden surface, creating texture and interest.

DEALING WITH RAW, UNTREATED SURFACES

Even if the chosen piece of furniture is unpainted it is still important to ensure that the surface is clean and dust free, and to smooth any rough edges with sandpaper. Furniture which is made from real wood, that is, not pressed wood (also called fiberboard or particleboard) or plywood, can be scrubbed with mineral spirits to open up the wood grain. To do this, pour some mineral spirits onto the raw wood and scrub in the direction of the grain with a wire brush. After this treatment it will be important to clean off the mineral spirits with warm soapy water if the decorative work is to be executed in acrylics.

CREATING A NEW LOOK

All kinds of choices can be made for changing features on a piece of furniture, such as changing existing handles or adding moldings and extra beading. Texture and interest can also be added to the surface by using a chisel and nails to distress the piece to give an authentic weathered look.

PRIMING AND BASE COATS

Priming and base coats are important to seal the surface. Oil-based paints have separate undercoat paints which are thinner than their oil-based top coats and easier to apply. They not only seal the surface to prevent the top coats from sinking into the wood and drying dull and patchy but also help to obtain an even top coat which should only require one application. Acrylic, water-based paints do not require a separate undercoat; watered down they will act as their own undercoat and primer. This first coat will sink into the wood and seal the surface. Once dry, this first coat can be followed by a coat of the same paint undiluted. If the furniture has a good, smooth existing coat of paint then again determine whether it is oil- or water-based. If it is water-based then an immediate change of color can be made with an oil-based or water-based paint. If the existing coat is oil-based, then only a further coat of oil-based paint can be immediately applied without first keying the surface.

Apply a priming coat to seal the wood and to help obtain an even top coat.

Determine whether an existing coat is oil- or water-based before applying a fresh coat.

METHODS FOR DISTRESSING PAINT

There are various ways of distressing or achieving a distressed look with paint, some of which are utilized on projects contained in this book.

SANDING: After priming with the undiluted acrylic paint and applying a solid base coat of the same color, add further coats of contrasting shades of acrylic paint and, when dry, sand areas and edges to give an excellent multi-tone distressed background to further motif work (see American Craft Chair).

WIPING: Apply primer coat and base coat in acrylic paint then, in a contrasting shade, apply another coat of acrylic paint in sections, brushing the paint on in the direction of the wood grain, i.e. across the top down the sides. Before the paint is dry, wipe off streaks of paint to expose the underlying color (see Italian Fresco-style Cabinet). This effect gives a strong distressed, dragged look.

WATER ON OIL: This distressing technique breaks all the rules mentioned about not putting acrylic paint over oil! Apply an oil-based primer and a base coat of semi-gloss oil-based paint, allowing each to dry. Now apply a coat of acrylic paint. Be generous with the paint and work in the direction of the wood grain so that the paint dries in ridges of dragged paint. Allow to dry, and wipe away areas of the thinner acrylic paint with a cloth soaked in denatured alcohol. The denatured alcohol will only remove areas of acrylic paint; the oil-based base coat will remain intact. Because of the rule of not putting acrylic on top of an oil-based paint, this method will need protecting with a couple of coats of a good oil-based varnish.

STRIPPING: Existing, old layers of paint can be stripped and sanded in desired areas for a genuine distressed look. Also experiment with blobs of beeswax in chosen areas on old layers of acrylic paint. Allow the beeswax to sit on the paint for at least ten minutes and then remove with a cloth. The beeswax will have eaten through the layers of paint.

LIMING: Liming wax is a white oil-based wax which is applied to wood with a good grain. Open up the wood grain with the mineral spirits and wire brush technique (see above). The liming wax can be applied to the raw, scrubbed wood or a coat of wood stain or acrylic paint can be applied as a base coat. Wood stains are available in oil-based or acrylic. If an oil-based wood stain is used then cleaning the wood with warm water and detergent will not be necessary; but if using water-based wood stain or paint, the mineral spirits will need to be cleaned off. Acrylic base colors which work particularly well under liming wax are terracotta, blue, green and black. Once the base coat is dry, apply a generous layer of liming wax with a brush, and work the wax well into the grain of the wood. Wait about five minutes and then remove any excess liming wax with a soft cloth. The result is a white grain to a wood or colored background.

DRY BRUSHING: This is an effective

After applying contrasting layers of paint, sand areas and edges for a distressed look.

Another way of distressing is to wipe off streaks of paint before it is dry.

technique to use on furniture with carved detail or moldings. Once a base coat of acrylic paint has been applied and allowed to dry, a lighter tone or white acrylic paint thickened with whiting (a fine white chalk) is used to highlight the molding detail. Dry brushing is achieved by having very little paint on the brush, and using a small flat fitch catch the edges of any detail with the thick, dry, lighter shade.

GLAZES AND ACRYLIC WASHES

GLAZES: Oil- and water-based glazes are available. The oil-based glaze has to be mixed with some oil-based undercoat paint to help the glaze set and to keep it from yellowing with age. It must also be diluted with mineral spirits to obtain easy and even application. Mix up the glaze as directed by the manufacturer. The glaze can be tinted by adding a little artists' oil color or universal tinting colors. Water-based glazes come ready mixed and are colored with artists' acrylic, acrylic tints or universal tinting colors. Experiment with the amount of dilution necessary for the chosen effect by slowly adding water.

ACRYLIC WASHES are a thin layer of acrylic paint which has been diluted. There is no set recipe to what degree washes should be diluted; simply experiment until you achieve the desired effect. Acrylic glaze can also be added to an acrylic wash to give the wash a glaze-like transparency and extra drying time. When acrylic glaze is added to an acrylic paint, the paint becomes glaze-like and can be softened with a softening brush (see Ribbons and Roses project).

FINISHING TOUCHES

VARNISHING: Oil- and water-based varnishes are available in all the finishes —matt, semi-gloss and gloss. Varnishes not only protect all the underlying artwork but also even out the finish. The choice of finish, including whether or not to tint the varnish, is made after all the decorative work is completed. For example, the design may benefit from a yellow tint to add warmth and age. This can be achieved by adding some oil color to an oil-based varnish or a little acrylic to a water-based varnish. Varnishing will always protect your work and is highly recommended for items which will be in constant use and prone to wear and tear. Varnish will protect furniture from sunlight and fading, water and water

Liming wax can be applied to raw or painted wood to emphasize the grain.

Varnishes protect surfaces and decorative work from fading, peeling and general wear and tear.

marks, condensation, and peeling and chipping. Varnish any item in contact with kitchens or kids twice for good measure. It is always a good idea to check the effect of a varnish on a test area first. Oil-based varnishes can have a yellow tint to them, so if no yellowing is desired (remember yellow varnish can make underlying blues look green), check that the varnish is clear or extra pale. Water-based varnishes have been known to dry misty or milky; sometimes this can be due to the climate, so varnish the piece in a well-ventilated, dry room.

POLISHING: Another way of sealing and protecting your work is by using French enamel or shellac. Shellacs are available in various tones, from blonde shellac, which is almost clear, to rich golden shellacs such as button polish, which is used for French polishing. Shellac will give the piece a lacquered look and the darker richer shellacs will add age and warmth. Many marbling artists use shellac to bring out the depth and colors in oil-based marbling. To obtain an even coating of shellac, pour the shellac onto the surface of the furniture where possible and spread with a soft brush. An aged mottled polish can be achieved by splattering the shellac with a little denatured alcohol, which will eat into the shellac and create mottled rings (see Italian Fresco project where colored shellacs have been used on glass).

WAXING: Waxing is also a way of protecting decorative work. A dark warm wax for woods such as walnut can be

Wax diluted with mineral spirits and rubbed or brushed thoroughly into wood grain gives a rich finish.

Shellac, or French enamel, will add depth and warmth as well as protection to a decorated surface.

Brushing antiquing fluid over decorative work gives an authentic "old" look.

diluted with a little mineral spirits and brushed into any wood grain, joins, chips and crevices and after five minutes, wiped with a soft cloth. This layer of wax will protect and again give the piece more age and character, and is particularly effective when worked into any molding or carved detail. Dark rich brown shoe polish can also be used for the same result.

ANTIQUING: Antiquing fluids create the same umber film over decorative work and can be used instead of a wax, but will need a coat of varnish over the top afterwards (see Autumn Leaves project).

BLOOMING: A bloom describes a milky film over underlying work. A bloom can be applied over acrylic artwork by mixing a cream acrylic paint with some water to produce a wash. This is brushed over the entire piece and worked in with a soft cloth until all the brush marks have disappeared and a smooth film of cream is left. This bloom will soften the underlying artwork and give the piece a faded look (see Poppy project).

SQUARING UP AND ENLARGING DESIGNS AND MOTIFS

Reference for designs and motifs can be taken from anywhere. Design and motif ideas are not usually the right size to trace and place immediately onto the piece of furniture, so some enlarging to the correct scale will often be necessary. One way is to have a color copy made of the design and have it enlarged on a copying machine, but sometimes the ratio is easier to work out by squaring up the reference. By squaring up the design any size can be decided on. Measure the area intended for the painted design on the furniture and the area of the original. Now divide the two areas into the same amount of squares; it does not matter what size the squares are on each area as long as there are the same number across and down over the area of the original and the proposed site of the new design. Either pencil in the grid of squares over the original or place a piece of tracing paper over the design and draw the grid onto this. Chalk can be used to draw the grid on the furniture. Now number the squares from one to however many squares along the top and bottom and up the sides of the grid, making sure that both grids are numbered identically. The grid will give a reference for enlarging the same design by following square by square on the original onto the larger squares on the chosen area on the furniture.

Blooming is a technique that uses a pale wash over an underlying color to create a soft faded appearance.

Antiquing fluids add a mellow tone but do not protect, so brush on a coat of varnish afterwards.

TABLES AND CHAIRS

TABLES, LARGE OR SMALL, ARE OFTEN THE FOCAL POINT OF A ROOM. ALL THE DESIGNS FEATURED IN THIS CHAPTER ARE SYMMETRICAL AND LOOK GOOD FROM ANY ANGLE. THE BORDERS AND SMALLER MOTIFS CAN BE ADAPTED TO DECORATE MATCHING FURNITURE. THERE ARE ALSO THREE STRIKINGLY DIFFERENT DESIGNS, IN TRADITIONAL AND BOLDLY MODERN STYLES, TO ENLIVEN A PLAIN CHAIR.

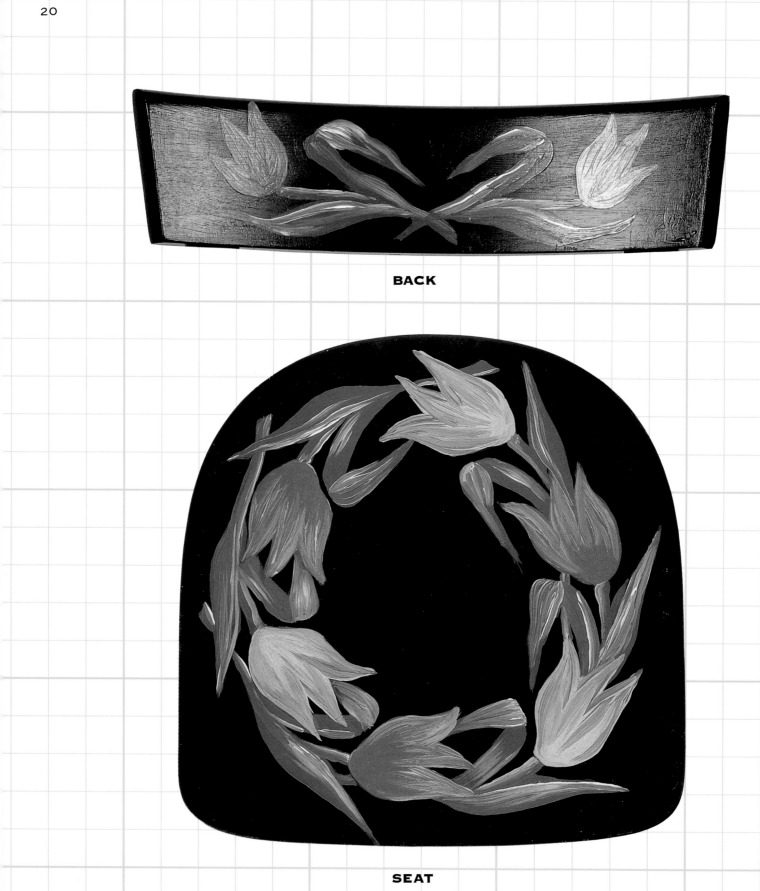

BACK

SEAT

Use the grid, following the instructions given on page 17, to draw up and scale the design to fit your chosen piece of furniture.

GYPSY TULIPS CHAIR

A SIMPLE, BOLD FUN WAY OF PAINTING AND AN EXCELLENT WAY TO
BRING TO LIFE AN OLD JUNK PIECE OF SIMPLE FURNITURE.

YOU WILL NEED

- *2in (5cm) decorating brush*
- *Black acrylic paint*
- *Tracing paper*
- *Pencil*
- *Chalk stick*
- *Red acrylic paint*
- *Yellow acrylic paint*
- *Green acrylic paint*
- *White acrylic paint*
- *Two small pointed brushes*

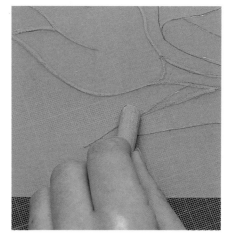

1 Apply a solid black acrylic base coat with a 2in (5cm) brush. You may need to apply a second coat for complete coverage.

2 Design a simple flower with a strong, pleasing outline. Trace the design onto a sheet of tracing paper with a pencil. Flip the tracing paper over, and trace the back of the design with chalk.

This vibrant design can also transform a plain chest of drawers.

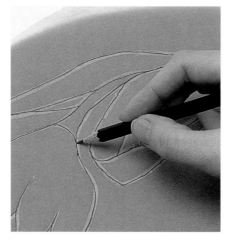

3 Place the tracing onto the chair seat chalk side down, and re-trace the pencil outline, transferring the chalk lines onto the chair seat.

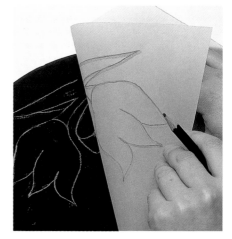

4 Carefully peel back the tracing and reposition it further around the chair seat. Aim to have an even amount of repeated flowers by the time the last flower overlaps the first. Trace two flowers onto the chair back.

5 When the tracing has been completed, wipe away any unwanted lines so that each flower appears to lie under the previous one.

6 With a small, pointed brush, block in flowers and stems in flat primary colors of red, yellow and green, alternating the red and yellow flower heads. When painting on black, two coats of the red, yellow and green will probably be needed.

7 When solid colors have been obtained on the flowers, wipe away the chalk lines with a damp cloth.

8 Now work with wet paint. With one small brush, reapply yellow paint to a yellow flower and, with the other brush, immediately apply streaks of red. Work all the yellow flowers this way, then switch to the red flowers, reapplying the red and streaking with yellow.

9 Use the same technique on the leaves. Reapply green to each leaf and immediately streak with white.

BASKET WEAVE COFFEE TABLE

BASKETS OR ANY WOVEN PIECES OF FURNITURE HAVE A LOVELY, NATURAL EARTHY LOOK TO THEM. WITH THIS BASKET WEAVE TECHNIQUE YOU HAVE ALL THE ADVANTAGES OF THE REAL THING BUT NO CATCHING, BREAKING OR CLEANING PROBLEMS. HERE IS A BASKET WEAVE TABLE THAT NEVER GETS CRUMBS CAUGHT IN IT!

YOU WILL NEED

- Ocher tinting color
- White paint (semi-gloss)
- 2in (5cm) decorating brush
- Pencil
- Tracing paper
- Glaze
- Flat fitch (No 6)
- Soft cloth
- Raw umber tinting color
- 2in (5cm) dragging brush
- Clear semi-gloss varnish

1 Mix ocher tint into white paint for rich cream base coat and apply to entire table with a decorating brush. (Two coats may be needed if the wood is raw and very absorbent.) Allow to dry.

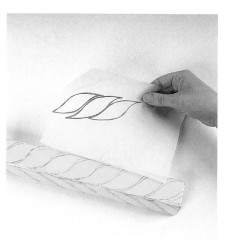

2 Draw a repeat pattern of diagonal "leaf" shapes on to tracing paper to fit the sides of the table legs and trace on to a leg face, top to bottom.

Use the same technique to create an authentic-looking basket weave chair.

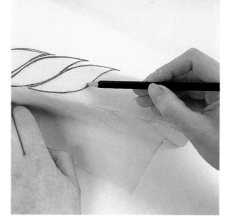

3 Reverse or slip the tracing on the adjacent leg face and back again on the 3rd face. This will make the shapes look as though they are woven into each other on each leg edge.

4 Mix ocher tint with the glaze and apply generously to entire leg face with the flat fitch, ignoring the tracing.

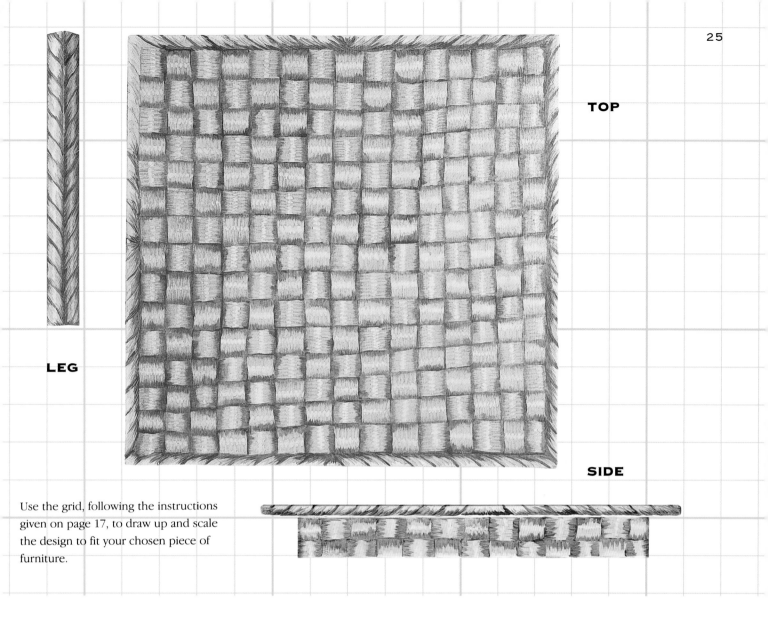

TOP

LEG

SIDE

Use the grid, following the instructions given on page 17, to draw up and scale the design to fit your chosen piece of furniture.

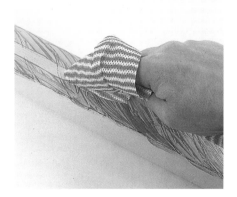

5 With a finger behind a soft cloth, wipe away a line of glaze down the middle of each leg face.

6 With a firm, flat fitch (No 6), brush the glaze back into the center making strong basket weave lines in the glaze and breaking up the wiped line, but leaving the center of each leg face clear of glaze.

7 Mix up more glaze with ocher and add raw umber tint. Apply this "shadow tone" glaze following the traced shapes, and brush the dark color in from the sides of each leg face.

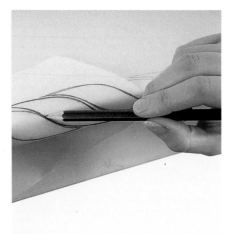

8 To emphasize the highlights down the center of the leg faces, dry brush (using very little paint) a small amount of white added to the original base coat.

9 Use the same tracing around the table top so that the highlight falls on the edges.

10 Using the same mid tone, ocher glaze, apply the glaze with a 2in (5cm) dragging brush. Drag the glaze in squares, alternating the direction of the drag on each square.

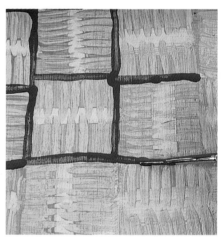

13 Apply a generous line of the dark, "shadow tone" glaze around each square.

11 After 10–15 squares, wipe out the center of each square, across the direction of the dragging lines.

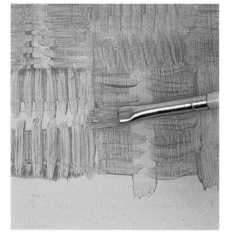

12 With a firm, flat fitch, brush the glaze back into the center of each square in strong basket weave lines. Break up the wiped line in places but leave the center of the squares clear of glaze.

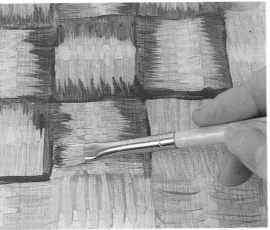

14 With a firm flat fitch, feather the dark glaze in towards the center of each square following the direction of the lighter glaze. Allow to dry and coat entire table with a clear, semi-gloss varnish.

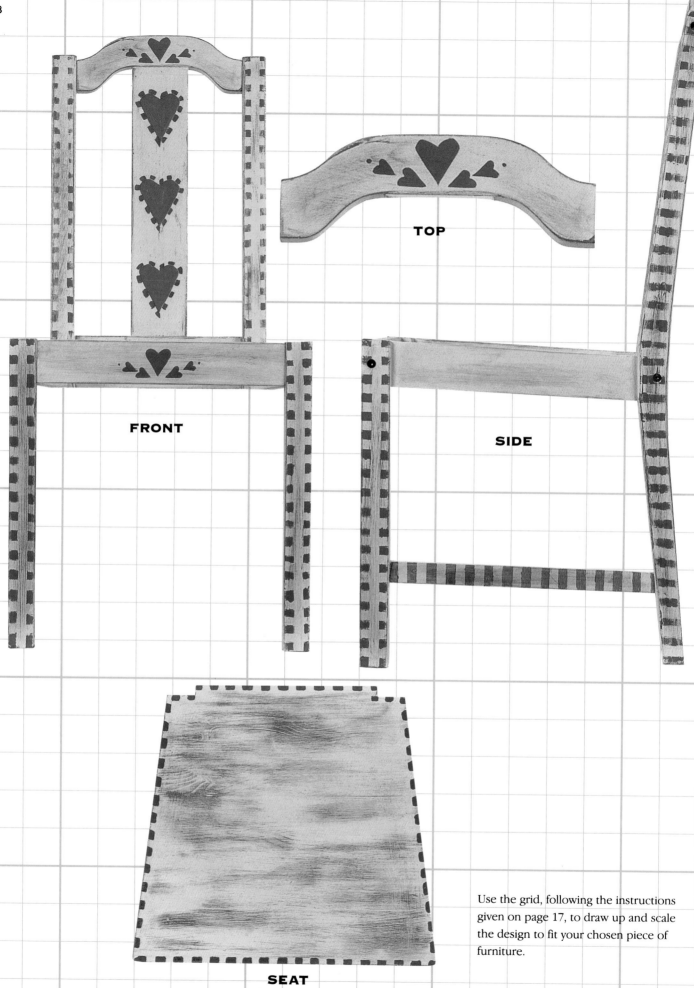

TOP

FRONT

SIDE

SEAT

Use the grid, following the instructions given on page 17, to draw up and scale the design to fit your chosen piece of furniture.

AMERICAN CRAFT CHAIR

THIS CRAFT-STYLE PROJECT UTILIZES ALL THE PRIMARY COLORS IN A TWO-LAYER DISTRESSING TECHNIQUE. A COLORFUL AND FUN IDEA FOR CHEERING UP ANY DULL, OLD WOODEN CHAIR.

YOU WILL NEED

- *1in (2.5cm) brush*
- *White acrylic paint (matt)*
- *Red acrylic paint (matt)*
- *Cobalt blue acrylic paint (matt)*
- *Bright green acrylic paint (matt)*
- *Yellow acrylic paint (matt)*
- *Medium grade sandpaper*
- *Tracing paper*
- *Pencil*
- *Small pointed brush*
- *¾in (2cm) masking tape*
- *Satin-finish varnish*

1 With a 1in (2.5cm) brush, seal the wood with a coat of white acrylic paint over the entire chair. Allow to dry.

2 Using the same size brush, paint the legs and outside back supports with red acrylic paint. Allow to dry.

Use this cheerful theme to revitalize a small cupboard for the kitchen or bathroom.

BACK

3 Paint the seat and the central back panel with the cobalt blue acrylic paint. Allow to dry.

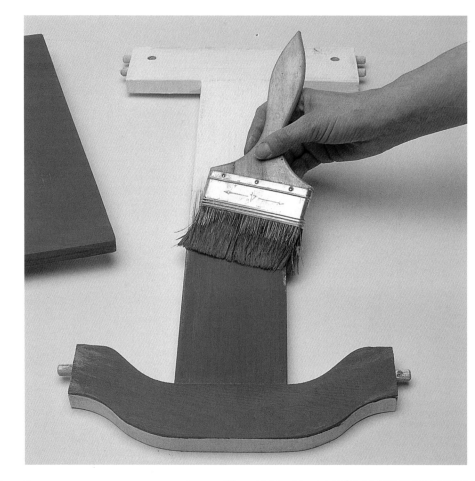

4 Paint all the remaining cross bars with the bright green acrylic paint. Allow to dry.

5 Now paint the entire chair with the yellow acrylic paint and allow to dry completely.

6 With a piece of medium grade sandpaper, lightly sand some areas so that all the base colors come back through the top yellow coat. Pay particular attention to the edges as this will bring out the design and shapes of the chair parts.

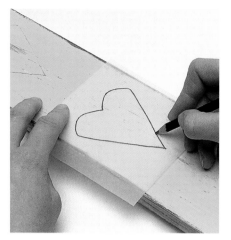

7 Draw a heart onto a piece of tracing paper and transfer onto the top of the central back support of the chair. Repeat two more hearts equally spaced underneath.

8 Using a small pointed brush, paint the hearts with the red acrylic.

9 Paint a broken line in blue acrylic around the chair seat border and the red heart motifs.

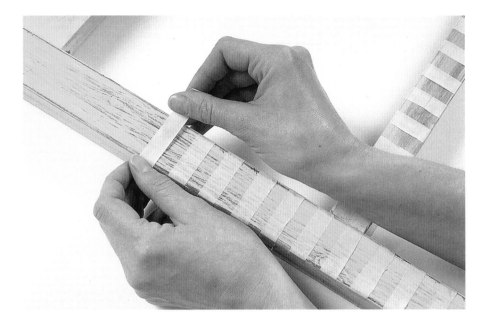

10 Apply strips of ¾in (2cm) masking tape across the legs and cross bars of the chair.

11 Apply a strip of masking tape down the middle of the legs of the chair.

12 On the legs paint all the unmasked areas in red acrylic paint and on the cross bars paint all the unmasked stripes in green acrylic paint. Varnish the chair to protect and prevent further, unwanted distressing.

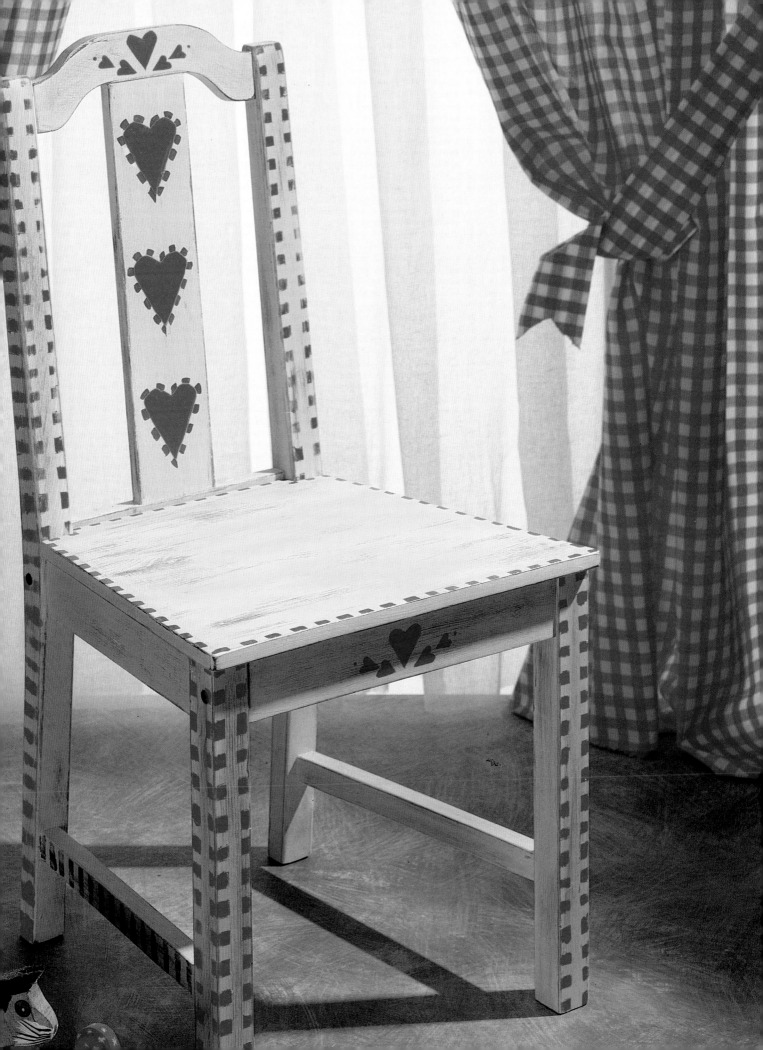

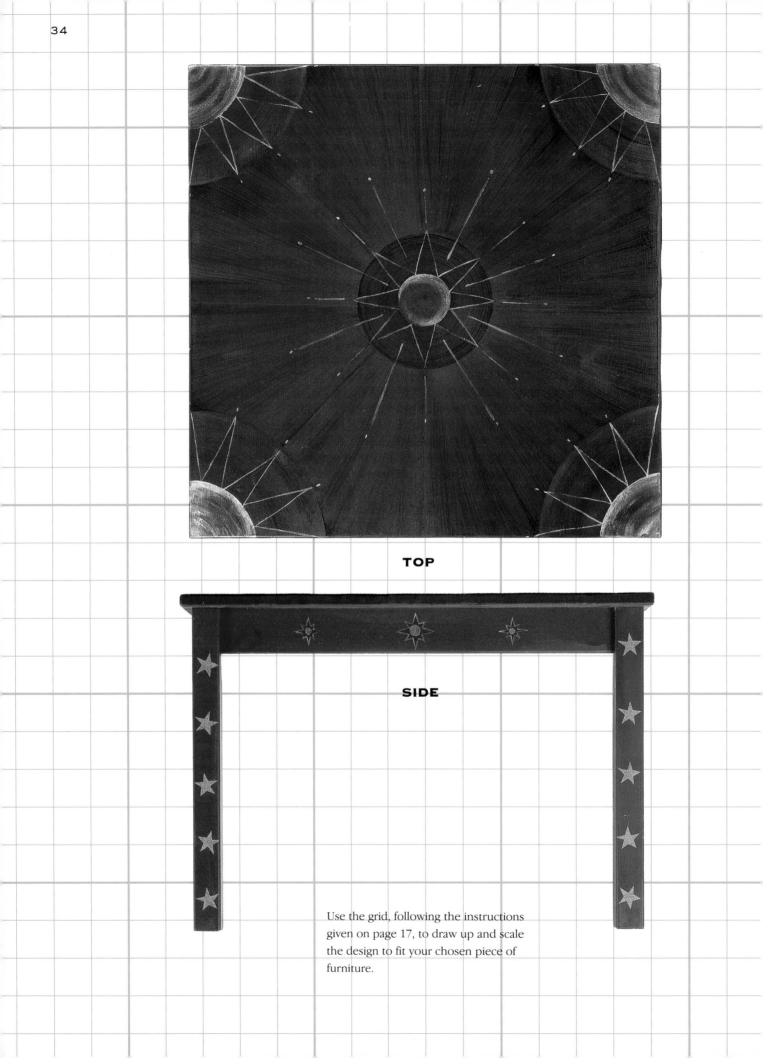

TOP

SIDE

Use the grid, following the instructions given on page 17, to draw up and scale the design to fit your chosen piece of furniture.

ART DECO TABLE

THE 1920S WAS THE ERA OF ART DECO, A TIME OF BOLD GEOMETRIC DESIGNS AND INTERESTING DECORATIVE WOOD EFFECTS ON FURNITURE. THIS DESIGN CAPTURES THE '20S WITH A '90S FEEL.

YOU WILL NEED
- *2in (5cm) decorating brush*
- *Rust/red acrylic paint*
- *Pencil*
- *Compass*
- *Acrylic glaze*
- *Black acrylic paint*
- *1in (2.5cm) brush*
- *4in (10cm) decorating brush*
- *Mineral spirits*
- *Small pointed brush*
- *Tracing paper*
- *Gold oil-based paint*
- *Satin-finish varnish*

1 With a 2in (5cm) brush, apply a base coat of rust/red acrylic paint to the entire table top and legs.

2 Divide the table top into quarters and mark the center point. Use a compass to mark a circle with a 5in (12.5cm) radius from the center point. Mark arcs of the same radius on each corner.

Continue the Art Deco look on a matching chair, or even a complete dining set.

3 Mix up a black glaze using equal amounts of acrylic glaze and black acrylic paint. Then, using a 1in (2.5cm) brush, apply the glaze to each corner arc on the table.

4 Using a large 4in (10cm) decorating brush, drag the wet glaze on arced sweeps across the corners of the table. Allow to dry.

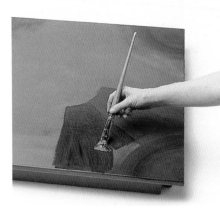

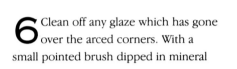

5 With a firm 1in (2.5cm) brush, drag the glaze from the edge of the central circle out towards the corners, working on each quarter panel at a time.

6 Clean off any glaze which has gone over the arced corners. With a small pointed brush dipped in mineral spirits, highlight the edges of the arced corners by bringing more of the base coat back through.

7 Using a firm 1in (2.5cm) brush, apply the black glaze to the central circle in concentric rings. You may want to practice doing this in one smooth motion so as to avoid any breaks in the circular, dragged lines.

8 Again using the firm 1in (2.5cm) brush, drag the black glaze along the side edges of the table top.

9 With a small pointed brush and black acrylic paint, define the arced corners from the other sections by feathering in the thicker black paint from the edge of each arc inwards.

10 Place a sheet of tracing paper over the central circle and a corner arc on the table top and with a compass, ruler and pencil measure out a sun design. Trace these suns through onto the table on the central circle and all the arced corners.

11 Using a small pointed brush, paint in the sun motifs in an oil-based gold paint, adding lines of gold radiating out from the points of the sun.

12 The oil-based gold paint can be blended into the underlying colors by working the paint out with a brush dipped in white spirit.

13 Add small star motifs down the table legs, using the oil-based gold paint. When all the paint is dry, protect the entire table with an oil-based satin-finish varnish.

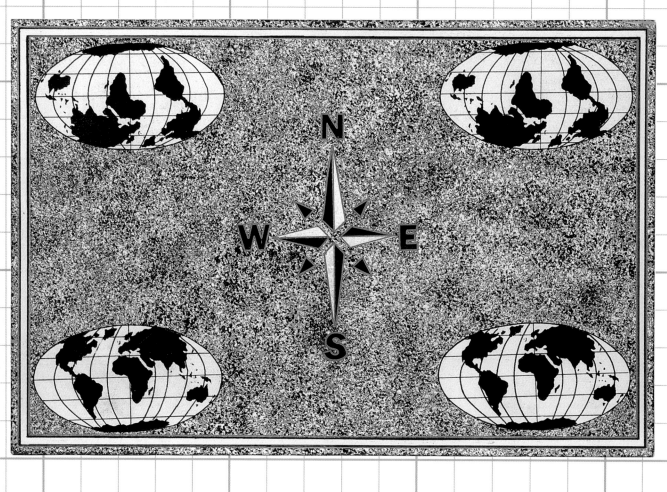

TOP

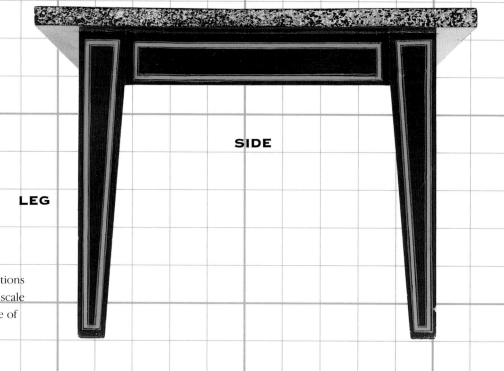

SIDE

LEG

Use the grid, following the instructions given on page 17, to draw up and scale the design to fit your chosen piece of furniture.

MAPS AND GRANITE TABLE

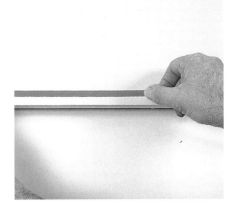

THIS DESIGN INCORPORATES AN EASY AND VERY EFFECTIVE GRANITE PAINT TECHNIQUE. THE CLEAN, SHARP MOTIFS LOOK INTERESTING AND EFFECTIVE OVER THE BUSY, SPECKLED BACKGROUND. IT'S PERFECT FOR A BOY'S ROOM OR A STUDY.

YOU WILL NEED
- *Ruler*
- *3in (7.5cm) brush*
- *White acrylic eggshell or silk-finish paint*
- *Quarter-inch tape*
- *Black acrylic paint*
- *Craft knife*
- *A natural sponge*
- *Acetate sheet*
- *Black permanent pen*
- *Round stenciling brush*
- *Tracing paper*
- *Carbon*
- *Pencil*
- *Small pointed brush*
- *Gold permanent pen*
- *Varnish*

Make a matching chair with compass points and a map.

1 Mix a little black acrylic paint into some white acrylic eggshell or silk-finish paint to make a light gray. Apply two coats to the entire table, allowing the paint to dry between coats and after the second coat.

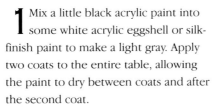

2 Measure ¾in (2cm) in from the edge of the table top and lay down strips of quarter-inch or 1cm tape all around the table.

3 Mix up a darker gray using the black and white acrylic paints. Sponge over the entire table top and edges using a natural sponge.

4 Sponge on black acrylic paint over the gray.

5 Splatter with slightly watered down white acrylic paint over the sponged area.

6 Using a small sharp blade, cut an oval template out of a sheet of acetate. Use the template to paint an oval on each corner of the table top, using the round brush and the light gray base coat paint.

7 Peel away the tape from the borders and outline the edges with a black permanent pen.

8 Trace a world map onto each oval using tracing paper and carbon.

9 Add longitude and latitude lines to the carbon tracing.

10 Paint in the map tracing with black acrylic paint using a small pointed brush.

11 Trace or cut a stencil for the compass from the template. Use the round stencil brush to pounce in with black acrylic paint.

12 Cut out and stencil in the compass points (N, S, E, W) in black acrylic paint. Divide each compass point in half and paint in white acrylic paint. Allow to dry.

13 Accentuate an inlaid look by outlining the points on the compass with a gold permanent pen.

14 Use the tape to mask in a border around the legs and sides, placing it ⅜in (1cm) in from the edge. Cut the tape at the corners with a small sharp blade or scalpel.

15 Paint the legs and sides with black acrylic paint, allow to dry and remove tape. Outline the white strips with a gold permanent pen. Varnish the entire table to protect it.

Use the grid, following the instructions given on page 17, to draw up and scale the design to fit your chosen piece of furniture.

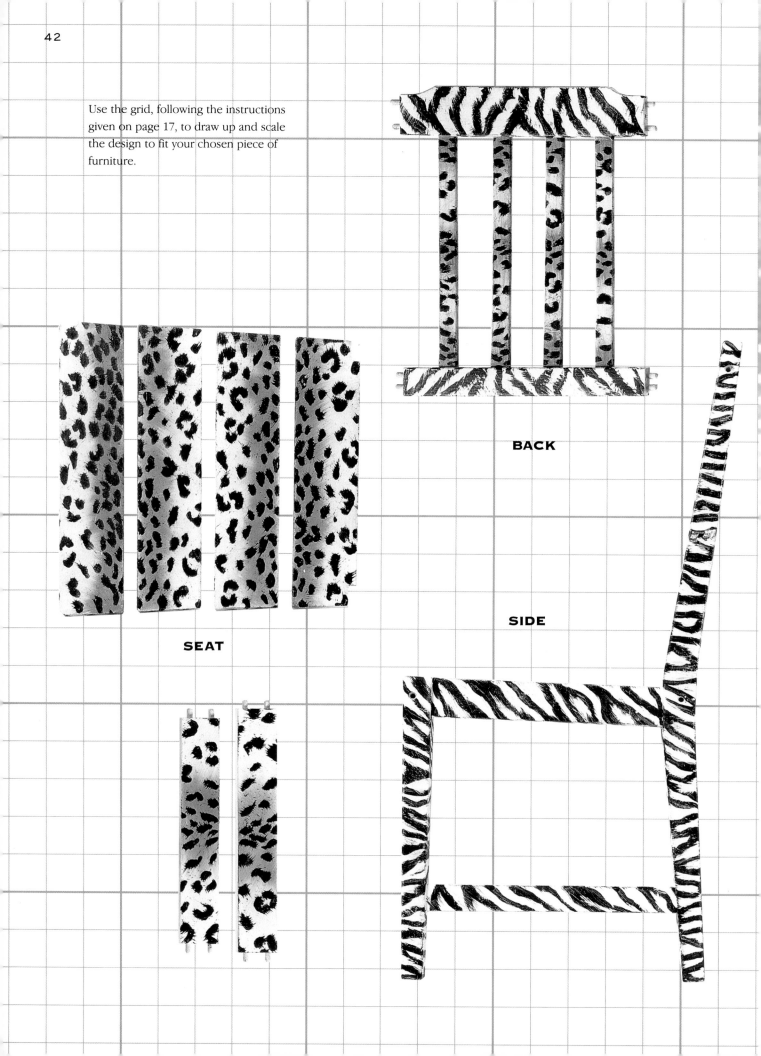

BACK

SEAT

SIDE

FAKE FUR CHAIR

FAKE FUR HAS ALWAYS BEEN FASHIONABLE. HERE IS A FAKE FUR PAINT EFFECT WHICH WILL TURN A PLAIN CHAIR INTO A STRIKING ACCESSORY TO GO WITH YOUR LATEST OUTFIT!

YOU WILL NEED

- *White paint, semi-gloss, satin*
- *2in (5cm) decorating brush*
- *Black acrylic tint*
- *Acrylic glaze*
- *Softening brush*
- *Small pointed brush*
- *Clear satin varnish*

1 Apply semi-gloss, satin white base coat to every section of the chair with the 2in (5cm) brush. Two coats may be needed if the wood is raw and very absorbent.

2 Mix up a gray glaze using the white base coat with black tint and glaze. Divide the leopardskin sections into equal panels of gray and white by first brushing a gray glaze in toward the white areas.

A bold splash of zebra stripes turns a plain table into a striking center piece for a room.

3 Apply a white glaze, brushing the glaze back into the gray areas.

4 Soften the glazes into each other with a softening brush.

5 With a black glaze and a small pointed brush, mark on a variety of leopard spots. Be generous with the glaze and paint the spots closer together in the center of the gray panels, spreading out to the white panels.

6 With the softening brush very lightly smudge the leopard spots. This is a minimal softening, just catch the glaze once or twice with the brush.

7 With the black glaze and a small pointed brush, mark on zebra stripes. Be generous with the glaze and use some reference for this, making sure the stripes are varied in their curves and joins.

8 With the softening brush very lightly smudge the black stripes.

9 Cover the white areas with a generous amount of white glaze.

10 Again, lightly smudge the white glaze back over the black areas with the softening brush. Cover the entire chair with clear satin varnish to finish.

TOP

Use the grid, following the instructions given on page 17, to draw up and scale the design to fit your chosen piece of furniture.

ROMANESQUE TABLE

THIS ROMANESQUE DESIGN USES AN ACRYLIC METAL LEAFING TECHNIQUE. THIS IS TODAY'S QUICK AND EASY ALTERNATIVE TO TRADITIONAL GILDING. TURN THE PLAINEST WOODEN TABLE INTO A NEO-CLASSICAL DINING TABLE FIT FOR A BANQUET!

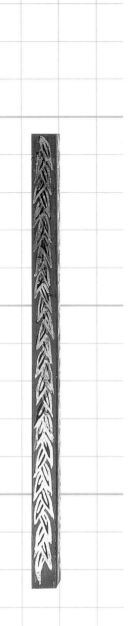

LEGS

YOU WILL NEED

- *2in (5cm) decorating brush*
- *Dark green acrylic paint*
- *Tape measure*
- *Pencil*
- *Masking tape*
- *Tracing paper*
- *Stencil paper*
- *Craft knife*
- *Chalk*
- *Black acrylic paint*
- *Small pointed brush*
- *Acrylic gold sizing*
- *Gold Dutch metal leaf*
- *Soft cloth*
- *Soft dusting brush*
- *Satin-finish varnish*

1 Apply just one coat of dark green acrylic paint with a 2in (5cm) brush. This single coat will sink into the wood and give a stained-like quality to the finish. Allow to dry. Measure out a 1½in (4cm) border around the table top.

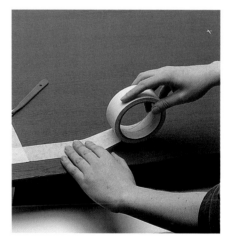

2 Mask the inside edge of the border with masking tape, rubbing the tape in well to prevent the paint from bleeding under it.

The Romanesque look can be applied equally effectively to drawer fronts.

3 On a sheet of tracing paper, draw a cross measuring the length and half the width of the chosen size of the central design. Now draw an arced line from the top of the cross to the end of the crossbar. Fold the tracing paper over and trace the arced line through so that the line becomes half an oval. At each end add the beginning of a curve going the other way. Then add leaf shapes along both sides of the line.

4 Copy the drawn design onto a sheet of stencil paper along with the central cross.

5 With a craft knife, carefully cut all the leaf shapes traced onto the stencil paper, and cut along the central guideline (along the length of the cross).

6 Measure to find the center of the table, and mark a cross with chalk. Lay the cutout stencil on the chalk lines, matching them up with the pencil guidelines on the stencil.

7 Paint the taped border using a 2in (5cm) brush and the black acrylic paint. Paint the stencil with a small pointed brush and the black paint. Allow to dry.

8 Paint over the black leaves with acrylic gold sizing. Outline the leaves with the gold sizing, leaving strips of black unpainted. Remember that any areas painted with the gold sizing will be gold.

9 With a 2in (5cm) brush, apply the gold sizing to the border and the edges. Leave irregular patches on the border clear of sizing; these will remain black and give a distressed look.

10 When the gold sizing is dry (when it is clear but still sticky), carefully apply sheets of gold Dutch metal leaf to the sized areas. Gently lay the sheets down and tear away any excess to reapply to the next area.

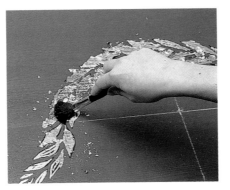

11 When the metal leaf has been laid down over the sizing, very gently smooth out any creases with a soft cloth. Be careful not to wipe the cloth over any exposed areas of gold sizing.

12 With a soft dusting brush, remove any areas of loose metal leaf within the design.

13 Apply the metal leaf in the same way to the border and edge of the table top, wiping the metal leaf away to expose distressed patches of black.

14 Turn the stencil around to the other side of the central cross, again lining up the guidelines on the stencil with the chalk lines on the table.

15 Stencil the new leaves in black acrylic paint, but pencil in the outlines of the leaves which go over or under the first stencil; paint these by hand.

16 Paint on the sizing, and add the metal leaf as before. Then, redefine any of the black lines on the leaves with black acrylic paint. Also paint in a stem running down the middle of the stencil.

17 With the black acrylic paint, carefully apply a little shading to make the leaves look as though one stencil is going over the other.

18 Using the same motif, but slightly enlarged, draw a trio of leaves onto a corner of a sheet of stencil paper and then apply to the table corners, following steps 5, 7, 8, 10, 11 and 12. Finish with a row of dots between the leaves, painted with the black acrylic paint.

19 Repeating the same sized leaf shapes as used on the central design, this time draw them onto a piece of stencil paper in a straight line to the length of the table legs and again repeat steps 5, 7, 8, 10, 11 and 12. Finally, when all decorative work is dry, protect the entire table with a satin-finish varnish.

SHELVES AND DRAWERS

The motifs chosen here are designed to work with the shape of the furniture, and to be effective as repeat patterns, for example on drawer fronts. Two-tone color washing, and stain or glaze techniques add interest to the design backgrounds. For a child's room, there is a bright circus-theme unit and, to delight a young girl, the selection is completed with a charming rose-strewn headboard.

TOP

DRAWER

SIDE

Use the grid, following the instructions given on page 17, to draw up and scale the design to fit your chosen piece of furniture.

POPPY CHEST OF DRAWERS

THIS GRAINED-EFFECT CHEST OF DRAWERS IS PAINTED IN PASTEL
SHADES, THEN FINISHED OFF WITH A BORDER OF DELICATE POPPIES.
YOU COULD USE FLAT-PACK FURNITURE FOR THIS PROJECT OR
REVAMP A PIECE OF FURNITURE THAT YOU ALREADY OWN.

YOU WILL NEED
- *Sandpaper*
- *Acrylic paint (blue gray, yellow ocher, black or dark brown, cream or white)*
- *Paintbrushes, No 3 and 4*
- *Pencil*
- *Ruler*
- *Soft cloth*
- *Chalk*
- *Walnut wax*
- *Ocher artists' acrylic*
- *Mineral spirits*

A small bedside cabinet would look charming painted in a pastel shade and scattered with poppies.

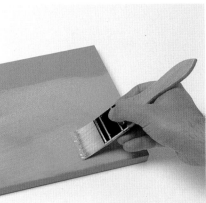

1 Rub down with sandpaper, then paint each panel in a solid base coat of acrylic; ocher, umber, or wood colors are ideal for a distressed look. With a pencil, mark out panels as guidance for your design around the drawers and the top of the chest of drawers.

2 Here gray has been used for the background of the design, but any color can be used. Water down the acrylic to two parts paint to one part water. Paint a section at a time, working the paint along the wood grain, not against it. After applying the acrylic, use a soft cloth to wipe the wash away exposing the base color.

3 Mark out the borders and paint yellow ocher on top. Next, mix the acrylic paint several shades lighter and continue with the same process around the borders, working the paint in the direction of the wood grain as before.

4 Sketch out a design to place in the corners of the panels. This can be repeated on all sides and a section can be used for smaller areas, such as the drawers. When you are happy with your design, either square it up or enlarge on a photocopier. Using pencil or chalk, make a tracing of the design onto the furniture.

5 Block the design in using flat mid-tone colors. Mix the mid-tone color with black or dark brown to darken it, and do the same with lighter colors, i.e. white or cream to lighten it. Now you have a mid-tone, a shadow color and a highlight color.

6 Decide where you are going to highlight your design (usually from the center or above). Work all three shades together so that you can roughly blend them together.

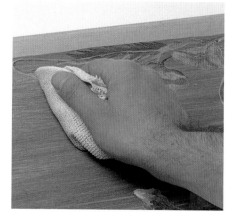

7 Add in the finer details of the design. When the painting is dry, lightly sand away areas of your design, especially areas on the exposed ocher base, so that a distressed quality is revealed.

8 Water down some cream acrylic and brush it over the whole area. Wipe the paint off quickly using a soft cloth leaving only a film of paint. This will give the base painting a faded quality.

9 Walnut wax, ocher artists' acrylic and mineral spirits can be used if you want the piece to appear antiqued. Again, paint it on and then quickly wipe it off leaving a subtle film of color. Finally, assemble your furniture.

58

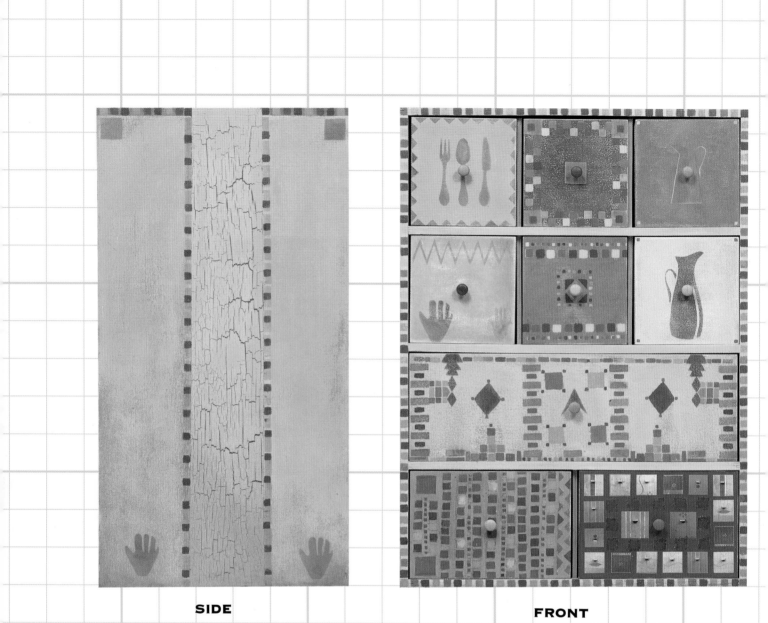

SIDE

FRONT

TOP

Use the grid, following the instructions given on page 17, to draw up and scale the design to fit your chosen piece of furniture.

MOSAIC
CHEST OF DRAWERS

A VARIETY OF TECHNIQUES ADDS COLOR AND INTEREST TO THIS VERSATILE CHEST OF DRAWERS. YOU CAN USE PURCHASED STENCILS TO FOLLOW THE MOTIF SCHEME ILLUSTRATED HERE, OR CREATE YOUR OWN FOR INDIVIDUAL EFFECT.

YOU WILL NEED
- Sandpaper
- 1–2in (2.5–5cm) decorating brushes
- Flat or semi-gloss paint in a selection of colors
- Decorator's sponge
- Stencils
- Brayer (or a radiator roller head)
- Colored paper
- PVA glue
- Matt-finish oil-based varnish
- Small stencil brush
- Masking tape
- Eggshell-finish paint (crackleglaze base color)
- Spackle (Polyfilla)
- Hair dryer or hot air gun
- Varnishing brush

Build up a bright mosaic of stenciled patterns on the top of a coffee table.

1 Prepare the unit by rubbing it down with sandpaper and brushing on one coat of latex paint. Allow to dry. Sand again lightly and apply another coat.

2 With a sponge, apply a wash of watered down latex paint (2 parts water to 1 part paint) to the top, sides and drawer fronts, varying the colors according to your chosen scheme. Allow to dry and then sandpaper lightly.

3 On a drawer front, stencil in your first motif with latex paint, using a sponge or brayer.

4 Stencil in a border around the edges of the drawer. When the paint is dry, lightly sand down.

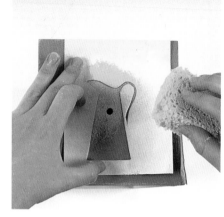

5 Working on the second drawer, apply another motif; this one will have a two-tone effect. Stencil in the first of your chosen colors.

6 When the paint is dry, reposition the stencil slightly and over-stencil with another color.

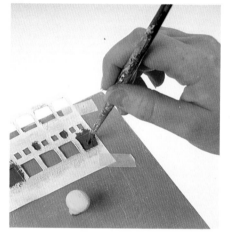

7 For the next drawer, cut out squares of colored paper and fasten them onto the drawer front with PVA glue, smoothing them down firmly.

8 After the glue has dried, brush on a coat of matt varnish over the paper squares to protect them.

9 Secure a mosaic-effect stencil to a drawer front with masking tape. Using a small stencil brush, fill in a selection of squares in one color only.

10 Without moving the stencil, fill in the remaining squares with a second color.

11 On the top of the chest, mask off a stripe with tape and using latex paint, wash color over with a sponge.

12 When the stripe is dry, mask off two more stripes on either side and paint with two coats of eggshell-finish paint in a contrasting color.

13 While the second coat of eggshell paint is still tacky, brush over a coat of latex paint in a lighter color, thickened with spackle (approximately 1 tablespoon to 2 tablespoons of paint).

14 Direct warm air from the hairdryer or hot air gun onto the top coat of thickened paint to encourage it to crack as it dries.

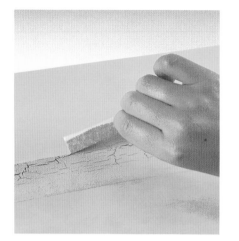

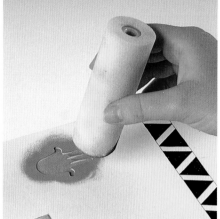

15 Peel off the masking tape when the paint is dry.

16 Continue to apply stencils to the top and sides of the chest, using a variety of motifs and applying the paint with a sponge or brayer.

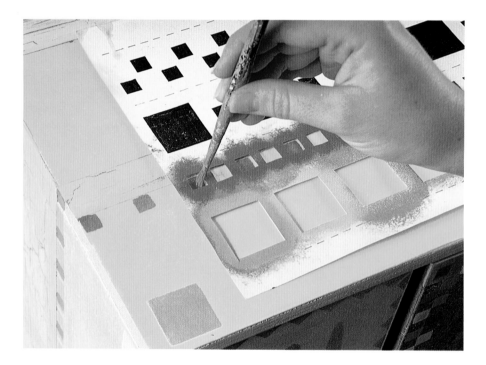

17 Edge the crackled stripes with stenciled squares, using a small stencil brush. Lightly sand down the whole unit to remove any remaining rough surfaces. Varnish the entire unit with two coats of matt-finish oil-based varnish, sanding lightly before applying the second coat and again when dry.

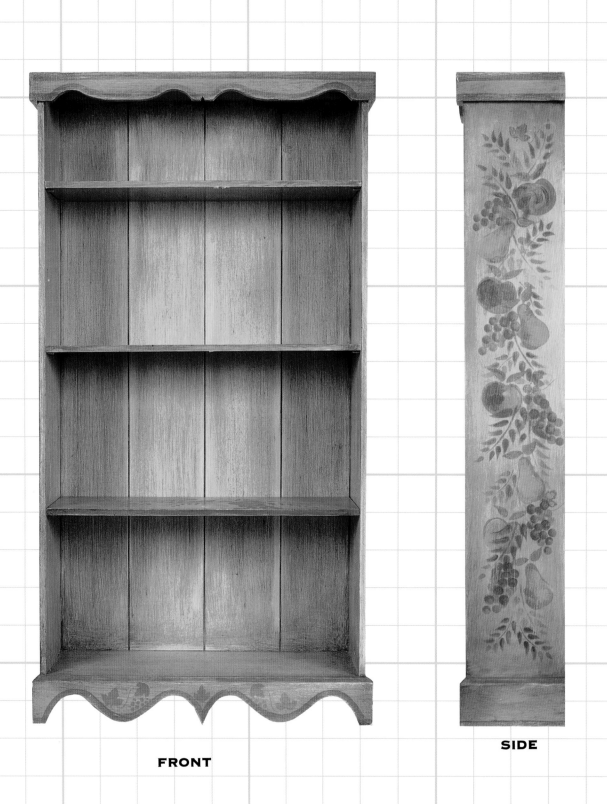

FRONT

SIDE

Use the grid, following the instructions given on page 17, to draw up and scale the design to fit your chosen piece of furniture.

SHELF

AUTUMN LEAVES BOOKCASE

THIS STENCILED DESIGN DEMONSTRATES HOW YOU CAN ACHIEVE AN INTRICATE MONOCHROME DESIGN BY BUILDING UP LAYERS OF THE SAME COLOR. THIS HAS BEEN DONE BY SIMPLY ALLOWING THE PAINT TO FADE IN SOME AREAS AND STRENGTHENING IT IN OTHERS BY OVER-STENCILING. FINISHED WITH AN ANTIQUING FLUID, THE FINAL EFFECT HAS AN OLD, SOFT DEPTH TO IT.

YOU WILL NEED

- *2in (5cm) brush*
- *White acrylic paint*
- *Rust, orange artists' acrylic*
- *Acrylic glaze*
- *Pencil*
- *Acetate paper*
- *Small sharp blade or craft knife*
- *Stenciling brush*
- *Sandpaper*
- *1in (2.5cm) brush*
- *Clear acrylic varnish*
- *Oil-based antiquing fluid*

Stencil this mellow design onto a lidded box to create a delightful "antique" look.

1 With a 2in (5cm) brush, apply a coat of white acrylic paint to the entire bookcase. Allow to dry.

2 Mix a rich rust colored artists' acrylic paint into some acrylic glaze and dilute with a little water. Apply as a color wash over the entire bookcase and allow to dry.

3 Design leaves and fruit shapes onto a sheet of acetate paper. Carefully cut out all the stencil shapes with a small sharp blade or craft knife.

4 Using the rust colored acrylic paint straight from the tube, stencil in the various leaf and fruit shapes on a randomly chosen design down the center of the sides, top and shelves. Allow the paint to run out and become fainter in places. Allow to dry.

5 With a sheet of medium grade sandpaper, distress the stenciled pattern in places to add to the "old" look.

6 Varnish the entire bookcase with a clear, matt acrylic varnish and allow to dry.

7 Apply a generous coat of antiquing fluid then brush the fluid into the underlying design with a 1in (2.5cm) brush.

8 Work the antiquing fluid out to achieve an even coat and to darken and age the finished piece.

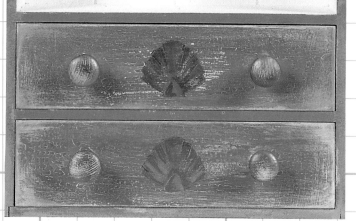

FRONT

SIDE

Use the grid, following the instructions given on page 17, to draw up and scale the design to fit your chosen piece of furniture.

DRAWER

FISH DESIGN BATHROOM SHELF

CRACKLE GLAZING IS AN EXCELLENT WAY TO ACHIEVE A BROKEN TWO-TONE BACKGROUND ON PAINTED WOODEN FURNITURE. TRY THIS SIMPLE DESIGN TO ENHANCE YOUR BATHROOM STORAGE AND SHELVING UNITS.

YOU WILL NEED

- *1in (2.5cm) brush*
- *White acrylic paint (matt)*
- *Acrylic crackle glaze*
- *Cornflower blue acrylic paint (matt)*
- *Sandpaper*
- *Stenciling acetate*
- *Craft knife*
- *Spray mount*
- *Silver gilding cream*
- *Copper gilding cream*
- *Oil-based satin-finish varnish*
- *Small pointed brush*
- *Raw umber oil color*
- *Flat fitch*

Surround a wood-framed bathroom mirror with the fish and shell motifs.

1 Using equal parts of water and paint, apply a watered-down coat of white matt acrylic paint to the entire unit with a 1in (2.5cm) brush. This diluted first layer will sink into the wood and act as a primer. Allow to dry.

2 Now apply a solid coat of the same white acrylic with no water added. Cover the entire unit and allow to dry.

3 Using a 1in (2.5cm) brush, apply a layer of acrylic crackle glaze to the front panel and drawers. To prevent drips, lay the crackled areas flat while the glaze is being applied and while it is drying. The more glaze used, the bigger the crackling. Allow to dry.

4 With the same size brush as before, apply a coat of cornflower blue acrylic paint over all the crackled areas plus the sides, top and shelf facing edges. Allow to dry.

5 With a fine grade sandpaper, lightly sand around the edges of each drawer and the front panel, i.e. all the crackled areas. This will expose the white undercoat, defining the edges of the unit.

6 Using stenciling acetate and a craft knife, cut out a simple fish shape. Spray the back of the stencil with a little spray mount and carefully place into the desired position on the top front panel of the unit. Apply silver gilding cream to the entire stencil with a finger.

7 With the stencil still in place, create some detail on the fish motif by applying areas of copper gilding cream, including a small copper circle for the fish's eye.

8 Apply silver gilding cream to all the drawer knobs until they have the appearance of solid silver.

9 Add touches of copper gilding cream to the knobs to give a slightly tarnished look.

10 Using stenciling acetate and a craft knife, cut out a simple scallop shell design. Spray the back of the stencil with a little spray mount. Place the shell motif onto the middle of each drawer front and define the shell divisions with some copper gilding cream, applied with a finger.

11 Add some delicate definition to the shell motifs using a fine, pointed brush and a little of the raw umber oil color.

12 With a flat fitch and the white acrylic paint, apply wavy lines down the sides of the shelving unit. This is a dry-brush look, so wipe any excess paint off the fitch before starting.

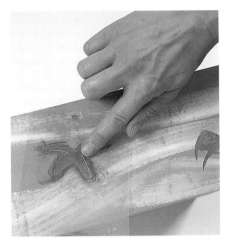

13 Again using the stenciling acetate and a craft knife, cut out a starfish motif and place on the sides of the unit, applying copper gilding cream with a finger. Also add the fish motif and some circles of copper, just with a finger, to look like bubbles.

14 With a flat fitch, apply more wavy dry-brushed white lines, going over the copper motifs. When the paint is dry protect the entire unit with an oil-based satin-finish varnish.

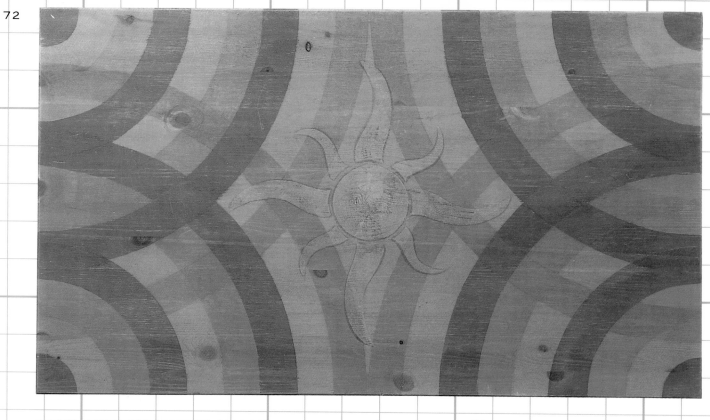

TOP

DRAWER FRONT

Use the grid, following the instructions given on page 17, to draw up and scale the design to fit your chosen piece of furniture.

SIDE PANEL

SUN AND CIRCLES DESIGN CHEST OF DRAWERS

THIS DESIGN UTILIZES THE NATURAL GRAIN OF THE WOOD IN COMBINATION WITH A WOOD-GRAIN EFFECT. NATURAL WOOD CAN BE STAINED ANY COLOR YOU CAN IMAGINE WITH ACRYLIC STAIN, SO WHY NOT EXPERIMENT WITH THIS IDEA OF MULTI-COLOR WOOD STAINING. YOU WILL DISCOVER HOW EFFECTIVE DIFFERENT BANDS OF COLOR FLOWING ACROSS LINES OF WOOD GRAIN CAN BE.

YOU WILL NEED
- *Tracing paper*
- *Carbon paper*
- *Compass*
- *Pencil*
- *Craft knife*
- *Clear acrylic glaze*
- *Blue artists' acrylic*
- *Yellow artists' acrylic*
- *White acrylic paint*
- *1in (2.5cm) brush*
- *Acetate paper*
- *Black marker pen*
- *Stencil brush*
- *Orange artists' acrylic*
- *Acrylic glaze*
- *Wood grainer rocker*
- *Matt-finish varnish*

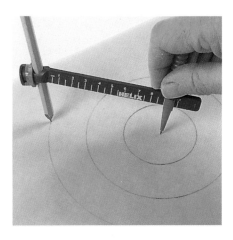

1 Design the circle shapes onto a sheet of tracing paper.

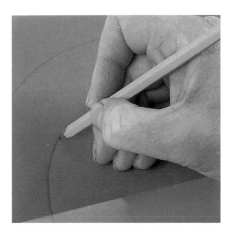

2 Using carbon paper, transfer the design straight onto the raw wood on the top, sides and drawer fronts of the chest.

This swirling sun and circles motif is perfect for the top of a round table.

3 Using a craft knife, carefully score along the traced lines to prevent the stain from running over the lines and into each other.

4 Pour some clear acrylic glaze into three separate containers. Add blue acrylic to the first, yellow to the next and both blue and yellow to the third. Dilute each with a little water. Apply bands of each color to the concentric circles.

5 Mix a little of the yellow acrylic into some white acrylic paint, and apply to the framework with a 1in (2.5cm) brush. Allow to dry.

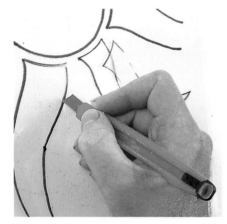

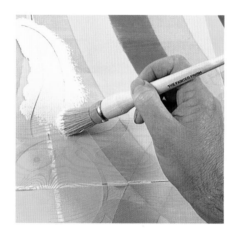

6 Trace a sun template onto a piece of acetate paper and carefully cut out the stencil with a craft knife.

7 Fix the sun stencil to the middle of the top of the chest, and stencil in the sun shape with a pale cream acrylic paint (use the same mix as for the framework but with extra white). Leave the stencil in position and allow to dry.

8 Mix a little orange acrylic into some acrylic glaze, and apply over the stenciled-in sun shape using a 1in (2.5cm) brush.

9 Add wood grain to the sun by dragging the rocker towards you without stopping until the rocker is off the stenciled shape. Allow to dry and varnish to protect with a matt varnish.

Use the grid, following the instructions given on page 17, to draw up and scale the design to fit your chosen piece of furniture.

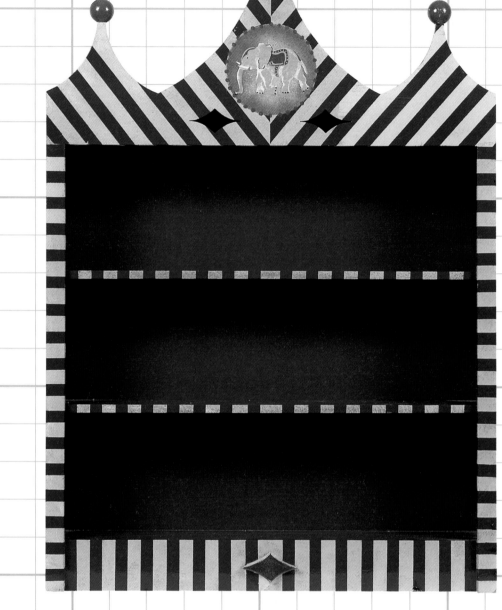

SIDE PANEL

FRONT

SEAL MOTIF

CLOWN MOTIF

CIRCUS DESIGN BOOKCASE

THE FUN SHAPE OF THIS CHILD'S BOOKCASE LENDS ITSELF TO A LOUD AND LIVELY DESIGN. BOLD STRIPES IN BRIGHT COLORS NEVER FAIL: THEY ARE FUN TO DO AND IMMEDIATELY CONJURE UP A CIRCUS FEEL. FINISH WITH INTERESTING STENCILS OF ANIMAL MOTIFS, ALWAYS A FAVORITE WITH KIDS.

YOU WILL NEED

- *2in (5cm) brush*
- *Royal blue acrylic paint*
- *Compass*
- *Acetate paper*
- *Craft knife*
- *Masking tape*
- *Spray mount*
- *Stenciling brush*
- *Yellow acrylic paint*
- *White acrylic paint*
- *Red acrylic paint*
- *Vivid, lime green artists' acrylic paint*
- *Tracing paper*
- *Pencil*
- *Carbon*
- *Small pointed brush*
- *Varnish*

1 Cover the entire bookcase with royal blue acrylic paint. Allow to dry, and apply a second coat if needed.

2 With a compass, draw seven circles onto a piece of acetate paper and cut them out with a craft knife. Keep the remaining acetate intact.

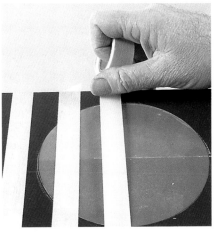

3 With a little spray mount, fix the circles to the sides and front of the bookcase. Tape over the circles with strips of masking tape, leaving an equal space between each strip.

4 Mix some white and yellow acrylic paint together and paint in the unmasked stripes. Allow to dry.

The circus design can be adapted to make a delightful toy-box.

5 Remove the strips of masking tape and the acetate circles.

6 Using the remaining part of the cutout acetate, paint in the circles with the yellow acrylic paint. Work in some red acrylic paint around the edges of each circle. Allow to dry.

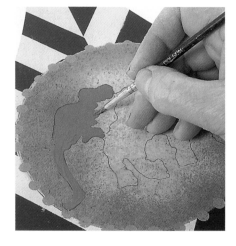

7 Stencil in vivid green dots around the edge of the main circle. Allow to dry.

8 Trace the outlines of a clown, seal and elephant from reference. Using carbon, trace the motifs onto each circle.

9 With a small pointed brush, paint in each figure by hand. Varnish to protect the bookcase.

TOP

DRAWER FRONT

SIDE PANEL

Use the grid, following the instructions given on page 17, to draw up and scale the design to fit your chosen piece of furniture.

SHELL DESIGN CHEST OF DRAWERS

THIS PRETTY SHELL DESIGN USES A GLAZE TECHNIQUE ORIGINALLY DEVELOPED FOR ACHIEVING A MALACHITE FINISH. BY SIMPLY WIGGLING A SOFT CLOTH OVER WET GLAZE YOU CAN ACHIEVE AN AMAZING AMOUNT OF DETAIL. IT MAY TAKE A COUPLE OF REHEARSALS, BUT PERSEVERE AND YOU WILL BE DELIGHTED WITH THE RESULTS.

YOU WILL NEED

- *2in (5cm) brush*
- *White acrylic eggshell or silk finish paint*
- *Ultramarine artists' acrylic*
- *Acrylic glaze*
- *Soft cloth*
- *Piece of cardboard*
- *Small pointed brush*
- *Dragging brush*
- *Acrylic gold sizing*
- *Aluminum metal leaf*
- *Satin-finish varnish*

1 With a 2in (5cm) brush apply a base coat of white acrylic paint. Apply a second coat if needed. Allow to dry.

2 Mix some ultramarine artists' acrylic into some acrylic glaze. Apply the glaze to a corner of the chest of drawers with the 2in (5cm) brush.

3 Fold a soft cloth into quarters, and fold it around a piece of cardboard. Starting at the far side of the area of wet glaze, carefully place the cloth-covered card on the glaze at an angle slanting towards you. Keeping the pressure constant, pull the card towards you across the glaze, wiggling the card up and down as you go. Don't stop until the whole shell has been completed; carefully lift the card off.

Alternatively, paint the shell pattern on a small cupboard.

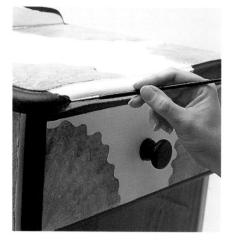

4 When a good shell has been achieved wipe away any excess glaze, leaving a clear wavy edge to the shell. Add shells to the sides, top and front of the chest. Allow to dry.

5 Using a small pointed brush, apply a coat of the ultramarine to all the borders around the top, sides, knobs and drawers. Allow to dry.

6 Add some white acrylic paint to the blue glaze and apply the lighter glaze to the remaining white areas. Use a dragging brush to do this, working in loose wavy lines which appear to weave over and under each other.

7 With the small pointed brush, coat all the dark blue borders and knobs with acrylic gold sizing. For a distressed look, leave random patches unsized; these will remain dark blue. Allow to dry (this is when the sizing is clear but still sticky).

8 Carefully apply sheets of aluminum metal leaf to the sized borders. When a border has been covered with the metal leaf, gently rub with a soft cloth to remove any loose pieces and expose the distressed blue patches.

9 Using the small brush, paint in a line of ultramarine around the inside of the silver borders. Allow to dry, and coat with a clear satin-finish varnish.

RIBBONS AND ROSES HEADBOARD

THIS TYPE OF DESIGN IS A POPULAR ANSWER TO WHAT TO DO WITH A GIRL'S BEDROOM FURNITURE. ROSES WILL ALWAYS LOOK PRETTY AND BE SUITABLE FOR A BABY BUT ARE ALSO SOPHISTICATED ENOUGH TO STAY A FAVORITE IN YEARS TO COME.

YOU WILL NEED

- *Pink acrylic latex paint*
- *2in (5cm) decorating brush*
- *Chalk*
- *Tracing paper*
- *Pencil*
- *Light blue and white acrylic latex paints*
- *Acrylic glaze*
- *Yellow acrylic tint*
- *Softening brush*
- *Small flat fitch*
- *Ocher, raw umber and red acrylic tints*
- *Small pointed brush*
- *Green acrylic tint*
- *Matt-finish varnish*

This charming design can be adapted very effectively for a bedside cabinet.

1 Apply a base coat of pink acrylic paint and allow to dry. Apply a second coat if needed. Locate and mark the center of the headboard, and divide the area into four with chalk. Lay a sheet of tracing paper on the headboard, aligning the corner of the tracing paper with the central point, and draw a wavy line. Trace the shape around the central point on each quarter to complete the central panel shape.

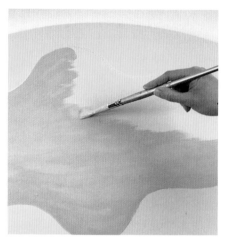

2 With a 2in (5cm) brush, fill in the central panel shape with light blue acrylic paint, and allow to dry.

3 Mix up three colors with acrylic glaze—a pale yellow, white and the blue panel color. Apply loosely and generously in cloud-like shapes over the blue panel.

4 With a softening brush, blend the paint and glaze mixes together to produce a soft sky effect. Allow to dry.

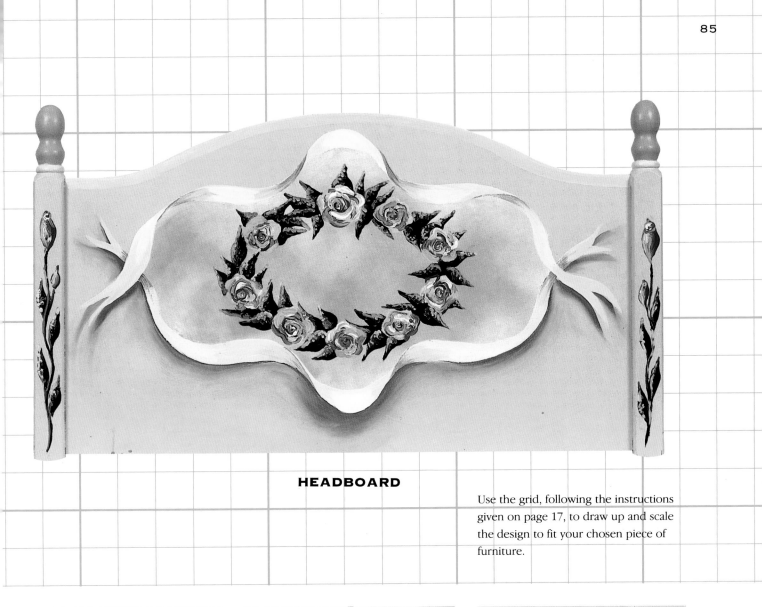

HEADBOARD

Use the grid, following the instructions given on page 17, to draw up and scale the design to fit your chosen piece of furniture.

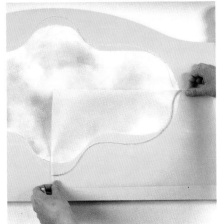

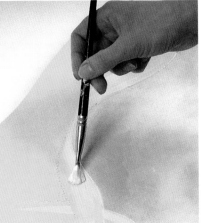

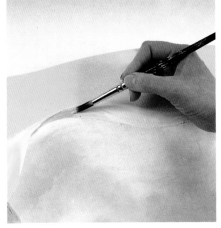

5 Take the panel shape tracing and trace it about 1¼in (3cm) below the original tracing on the two bottom quarters of the panel and 1¼in (3cm) above the original line on the two top quarters, creating a ribbon shape.

6 Mix some yellow tint into the white paint to make a light yellow. With a small flat fitch, mark in the ribbon areas in yellow, adding ribbon tail ends crossing over each other on either side of the clouded panel.

7 Add some ocher and raw umber to the light yellow ribbon color to create a shadow tone. Apply with a small flat fitch to sections of the ribbon which are in shadow, i.e. where the other ribbon crosses over the top or, where the ribbon twists on itself.

8 Darken a little of the pink background color by adding some red and some raw umber, creating a shadow color to apply under the bottom ribbon. Make the line thicker where the ribbon is wide and sitting away from the background.

9 Dip a 2in (5cm) brush into the original background color and blend the wet, dark pink shadow line to soften the shadow.

10 With a piece of chalk, mark in an oval shape in the middle of the clouded panel.

11 Use a small pointed brush and the pink base color to mark evenly spaced rose shapes around the oval.

12 Mix some green and raw umber to make a dark leaf green. Use a small pointed fitch to mark in leaves, completing the oval shape.

13 Re-apply the base pink tone to one rose at a time, then add the shadow parts of each rose with the darker pink shadow color and the highlights with white. Let the three wet tones go into each other in a very loose, streaky blend.

14 Lighten some of the dark leaf green with white. Re-apply the original dark green to a leaf at a time, this is the shadow tone for the leaves. Apply the lighter green as the midtone and then highlight with white. Again, allow the shades to merge into each other in places.

15 Use chalk to sketch a simple stem with leaves and buds as a side motif on the posts. Block in the dark green and pink.

16 Shade and highlight the side motifs in the same way as steps No. 13 and 14.

17 Finally, fill in any detail and a border with the light blue base and the yellow ribbon colors. Allow to dry, and protect with a matt varnish.

CABINETS AND CLOSETS

THIS CHAPTER DEMONSTRATES HOW TO DECORATE
LARGER PIECES OF FURNITURE SUCH AS A BUILT-IN
STORAGE UNIT, OR THOSE WITH SOLID, FLAT SURFACES.
BY MIXING UNUSUAL TECHNIQUES LIKE TROMPE L'OEIL,
PANELING OR PAINTING GLASS DOORS, YOU CAN CREATE
A DRAMATIC ILLUSION OF DEPTH, PERSPECTIVE,
AND TEXTURE.

SIDE PANEL

DOOR

Use the grid, following the instructions given on page 17, to draw up and scale the design to fit your chosen piece of furniture.

ITALIAN FRESCO-STYLE CABINET

A LOVELY EARTHY LOOK, IDEAL FOR KITCHEN FURNITURE. THE RUBBED-BACK STYLE IN WARM TUSCAN COLORS GIVES THE PIECE A FRESCO FEEL, AND THE PAINTED GLASS ADDS INTRIGUE AND INTEREST TO THE DOOR.

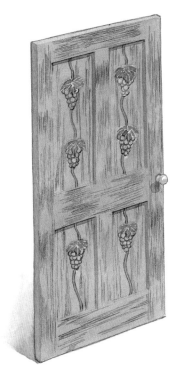

Follow this Mediterranean theme to decorate the panels of a door.

YOU WILL NEED

- *2in (5cm) decorating brush*
- *Red oxide acrylic paint*
- *1in (2.5cm) dragging brush*
- *Turquoise acrylic paint*
- *Tracing paper*
- *Stencil paper*
- *Pencil*
- *Craft knife*
- *White acrylic paint*
- *Ocher artists' acrylic*
- *Small pointed brush*
- *Olive green acrylic paint*
- *Raw umber acrylic paint*
- *Soft cloth*
- *Purple acrylic paint*
- *Red and blue or purple glass paint (these can be methylated or white spirit based)*
- *Dark brown glass paint*
- *Green glass paint*
- *Clear varnish*

GRAPE MOTIF

1 With a 2in (5cm) brush, apply a base coat of red oxide acrylic paint (two coats if required). Allow to dry.

2 With a 1in (2.5cm) dragging brush, apply turquoise acrylic paint in broken dragging lines over the red oxide. Follow the direction of the panels, i.e. across the top and down the side panels of the cabinet.

3 Design a grape and leaf motif measuring one third of the length of the cabinet side panels. Trace the motif onto a piece of stencil paper, adding the beginning of the next repeat. Carefully cut out only the leaf and vine areas of the stencil with a craft knife.

4 Center the stencil at the top of the side panel of the cabinet. Mix up some rich cream-colored emulsion using white with some ocher artists' acrylic and apply to all the cut areas of the stencil, including the beginning of the next repeat. Carefully lift the stencil and reposition further down for the next repeat. Allow to dry.

5 Using a small, pointed brush, paint in the first leaf with olive green acrylic paint.

6 Before the olive green has dried, rub with a soft cloth to expose some of the cream base. The edges of the leaf can be left the darker green. Move onto the next leaf and repeat the process.

7 Apply the same process to the vine areas using raw umber acrylic and wiping away the middle of the vine before the raw umber has completely dried.

8 Carefully cut out the rest of the stencil and place in position on the side of the cabinet. With a small pointed brush, paint in the grape area with the mixed up cream acrylic. Allow to dry.

9 Mix a little red oxide and raw umber into some purple acrylic; this will produce a burgundy which will tone in well with the other shades used. Apply the burgundy to the grape area and, before it has dried, use a soft cloth to wipe away a highlight on each grape.

10 Using the small brush, paint on some fine leaf veins with the cream acrylic.

11 Make a fresh stencil with just the leaf and vine areas cut out. Position it at the top center of the back of the glass door, and tape into position.

12 Paint the vine with a dark brown glass paint and the leaves with a mix of brown and green glass paint (this will be similar to the olive green on the acrylic leaves).

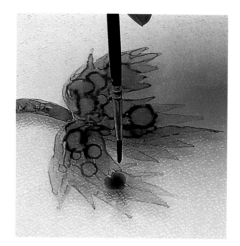

13 To add detail and interest to the glass leaves, load up the brush with the green glass paint and allow the paint to drop onto the leaf area. The ridge that the first coat will have left will prevent the paint from bleeding over the edge of the leaf shape.

14 Cut out the rest of the stencil and place back into position. Mix up some burgundy-colored glass paint (use red and blue or purple and a touch of the dark brown). Apply the burgundy glass paint to the grape areas.

15 Give the grapes more detail by reapplying more burgundy glass paint. Work the brush in circles to outline each grape; the glass paint will thin at the center and collect around the edge of each grape. Coat the glass door with a clear varnish to protect.

SIDE

LEFT DOOR

RIGHT DOOR

Use the grid, following the instructions given on page 17, to draw up and scale the design to fit your chosen piece of furniture.

THEATRICAL DRAPES CLOSET

SWAGS OF FABRIC ALWAYS SOFTEN A ROOM. THIS DESIGN WILL SOFTEN ANY ANGULAR CLOSET AND ADD GLAMOR AND FLAMBOYANCY TO YOUR BEDROOM.

YOU WILL NEED

- Chalk stick
- Tracing paper
- Pencil
- Measuring tape
- 2in (5cm) decorating brush
- Red acrylic paint
- White acrylic paint
- Black acrylic paint
- Two 1in (2.5cm) brushes
- Yellow/gold acrylic paint
- Small fitch
- Burnt umber artists' acrylic
- Acrylic glaze
- Soft cloth
- Satin-finish varnish

1 Take the doors off the closet before beginning. Using a chalk stick, draw an outline for the desired shape of the drapes straight onto one of the closet's doors, keeping to a simple outline.

2 Once you are happy with the basic outline, trace it onto a large sheet of tracing paper with the chalk. Now reverse the tracing and, with a pencil, trace a mirror image of the first outline onto the other closet door.

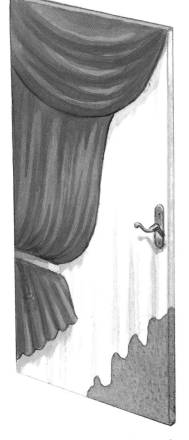

Add rich drapes to your bedroom door for a stunningly dramatic effect.

3 With a 2in (5cm) brush mark in the draped areas with a red acrylic paint, leaving a gap where the tieback would appear. Allow to dry.

4 Pour some of the red paint into two new containers. Mix some white acrylic paint into one container and some black into the other. Now you will have three shades: a pink, the original red and a dark red. Recoat a section of the curtain shape with the original red. Then, using a separate 1in (2.5cm) brush for each of the two new shades, apply bands of alternating pink and dark red in the desired direction of the folds.

5 Use a dry 2in (5cm) brush to blend the bands of color into each other, creating the look of soft folds. More of any of the shades can be added and blended immediately while the paint is still wet.

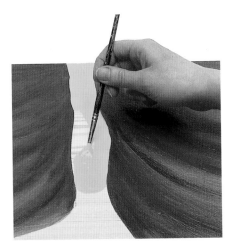

6 With a small fitch, apply a coat of yellow paint to the area left for the tieback.

7 Reapply another coat of yellow to the tieback if needed, and immediately streak some burnt umber acrylic into the wet yellow paint. The umber is the shadow tone, and should be applied at the top and bottom of the tieback and where the tieback disappears around the corner of the closet.

8 Use a dry 1in (2.5cm) brush to blend the burnt umber into the yellow, moving the blending brush vertically.

9 Mix some white acrylic paint into an acrylic glaze. Using a 2in (5cm) brush, apply the glaze mix onto the unpainted area of the doors.

10 Before the glaze is dry, use a finger behind a piece of soft cloth to wipe away lines of glaze, creating the look of folds in a transparent under curtain.

11 At the bottom of the white drapes, create folds in the material by wiping the glaze away in waves flowing down towards the outside bottom corner of the door.

12 Using a softening brush, blend the glaze into the stripes of background wood.

13 Mix a little black acrylic paint into the white glaze. With a small brush, apply the gray glaze in lines to create shadowy folds in the white curtain. Before the glaze is dry, soften the gray lines into the other areas. Allow to dry and varnish in a satin finish.

14 Tassels can be painted to complete the drapes, if desired. Use the same blend of colors as for the tieback (steps No 6, 7 and 8) and define the twists in the cords with highlight and shadow.

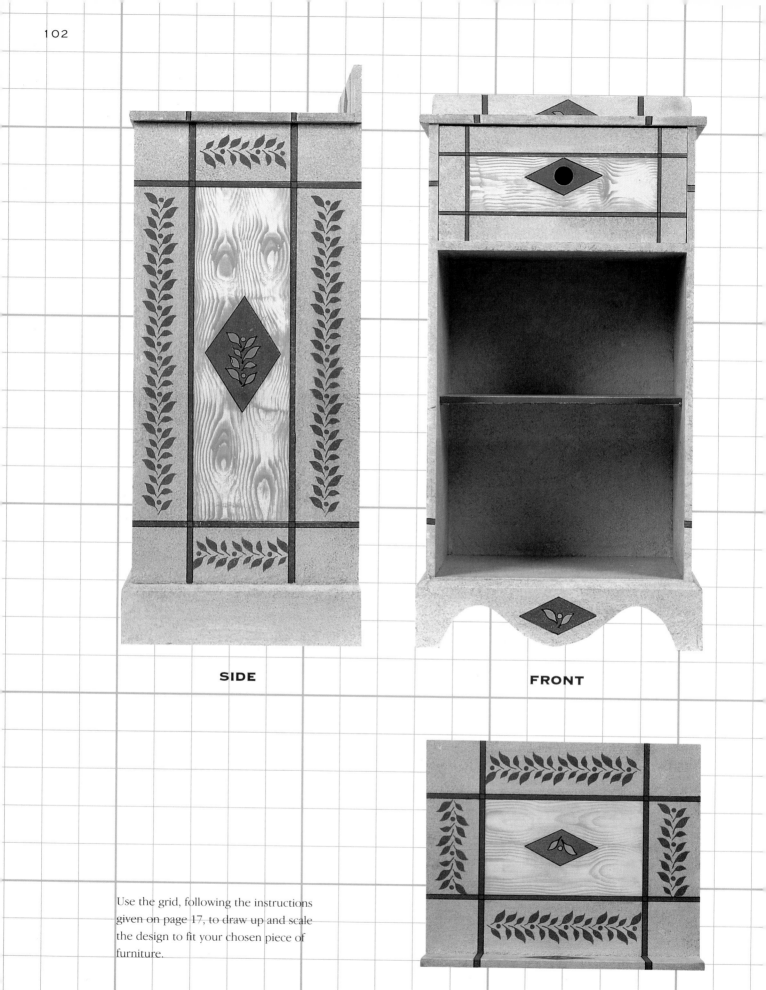

SIDE

FRONT

Use the grid, following the instructions given on page 17, to draw up and scale the design to fit your chosen piece of furniture.

TOP

DIAMOND MOTIF

SIDE

LEAF MOTIF

WOOD-GRAIN EFFECT BEDSIDE CABINET

GLAZE TECHNIQUES HAVE ENDLESS USES, AND THEY ARE PARTICULARLY EFFECTIVE AS BACKGROUNDS FOR DECORATIVE MOTIFS. THIS DESIGN INCORPORATES TWO DIFFERENT GLAZE TECHNIQUES. WITH THE ATTRACTIVE BORDER AND CENTRAL STENCILING EDGED WITH CLEAN FLAT LINES, THE END RESULT IS INTERESTING AND LOOKS BOTH PROFESSIONAL AND PLEASING TO THE EYE.

YOU WILL NEED
- *Ocher artists' acrylic*
- *White acrylic paint*
- *1in (2.5cm) brush*
- *Ruler*
- *Pencil*
- *Masking tape*
- *Craft knife*
- *Acetate paper*
- *Spray mount*
- *Dark green acrylic paint*
- *Stencil brush*
- *Acrylic glaze*
- *Rocker or wood grainer*
- *Low-tack tape*
- *Small pointed brush*
- *Permanent black pen*
- *Satin-finish varnish*

1 Mix some ocher acrylic into some white acrylic paint to make a warm cream color. With a 1in (2.5cm) brush, apply two coats to the entire cabinet, allowing each coat to dry.

The leaf and diamond motifs would add interest to the simple outlines of a wooden headboard.

2 Measure a 3in (8cm) border around the top and sides of the cabinet, and a 1¼in (3cm) border around the drawer. Mask the borders with tape.

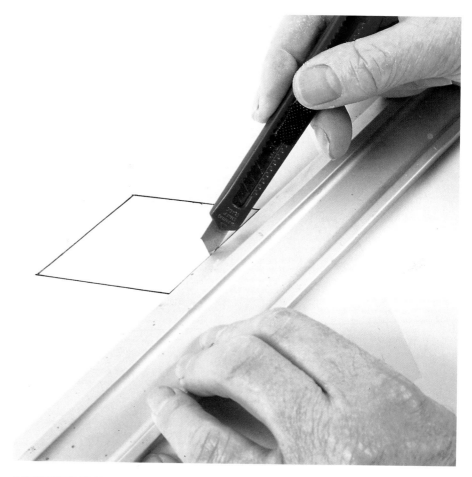

3 Draw a diamond shape onto a piece of acetate.

4 Use a sharp craft knife to cut out the diamond, leaving both the diamond and the remaining acetate intact.

5 Locate the center of the top and sides of the cabinet and with a little spray mount, fix the diamond surround acetate into position. Stencil in the diamond with the stenciling brush in dark green acrylic paint and allow to dry. Remove the acetate paper and fix the positive part of the stencil over the green diamond for protection during glazing.

6 Mix a little ocher acrylic into some acrylic glaze and apply to the main panel on the top and sides of the cabinet. Stipple the glaze to remove brush strokes and excess glaze, as very little glaze is needed for wood graining.

7 To achieve the wood-grain effect, use a wood grainer or rubber rocker in one movement without stopping. Start at the far side of the panel and drag the grainer towards you rocking it continuously backwards and forwards at the same time. Allow to dry.

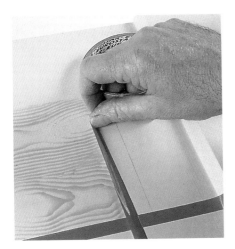

8 Remove masking tape from the edge of the wood-grained panel and retape the inside edges of the border using ¼in (1cm) low-tack tape. Run the tape off the edges so that the border has a square on each corner.

9 Mix a little dark green acrylic paint into some acrylic glaze and apply to every section of the border. Stipple the glaze to remove brush strokes and leave to dry.

10 Remove the low-tack tape and retape either side of where the tape was. Paint in an edging line in the dark green acrylic paint. Allow to dry and remove tape.

11 Copy the leaf design onto a sheet of tracing paper to fit inside the long border panels.

12 Trace the leaf design onto the long panels around the border.

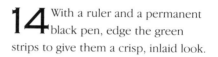

13 With a small pointed brush, paint in the leaf designs in the dark green acrylic paint.

14 With a ruler and a permanent black pen, edge the green strips to give them a crisp, inlaid look.

15 Trace a section of the leaf design onto the central diamond. Add some white to the dark green acrylic paint, matching the tone of the green stippled borders, and apply to the leaf design. Allow to dry. Edge the diamond and pale green leaves with the black permanent pen. Varnish with a satin-finish varnish to protect.

FRONT

SIDE

Use the grid, following the instructions given on page 17, to draw up and scale the design to fit your chosen piece of furniture.

HERB CUPBOARD

THIS ATTRACTIVE LATTICE-FRONTED CUPBOARD WILL BOTH STORE AND DISPLAY YOUR DRIED HERBS. THE MOTIFS USED HERE ARE BAY, ROSEMARY, MARIGOLD, CHIVE, AND BORAGE, BUT YOU CAN CHOOSE YOUR OWN FAVORITES.

YOU WILL NEED

- *2in (5cm) decorating brush*
- *White acrylic paint (matt)*
- *Yellow acrylic paint (matt)*
- *Terra cotta acrylic paint (matt)*
- *Turquoise blue acrylic paint (matt)*
- *Acrylic crackle glaze*
- *Soft cloth*
- *Bright orange artists' acrylic*
- *Pencil*
- *Tracing paper*
- *Low tack tape*
- *Ball-point pen*
- *Small pointed brush*
- *Mid-green acrylic paint*
- *Cobalt blue acrylic paint*
- *Lilac acrylic paint*
- *Dark blue acrylic paint*
- *Varnish*

Extend the herb theme on a plainer cabinet, enlarging a motif for emphasis.

1 Using a 2in (5cm) brush, cover the entire cabinet with a primer coat of watered down acrylic white paint, followed by a solid coat of undiluted white acrylic. This will give all the following coats more vibrancy. Allow to dry.

2 With a 2in (5cm) brush, apply one coat of bright yellow acrylic paint to the inside of the cupboard and door.

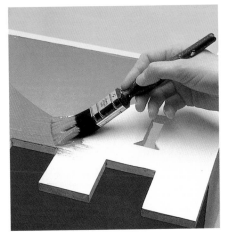

3 With the same size brush used in steps No. 1 and 2, apply one coat of terra cotta colored acrylic paint to the outside of the cupboard, but not the door.

4 Apply one coat of turquoise acrylic paint to the outside of the door and the return. Allow to dry.

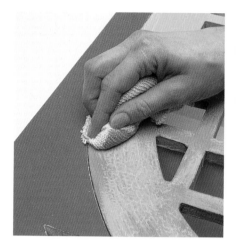

5 Apply a layer of acrylic crackle glaze over the turquoise blue area. To achieve larger crackling, apply more glaze; use less glaze for smaller crackling. Allow to dry.

6 Mix up some orange using equal amounts of the terra cotta and yellow acrylic paints; apply over the blue glazed area. Take care not to overbrush the paint so that the glaze is not disturbed. Allow to dry.

7 With a soft cloth, lightly apply some strong, orange artists' acrylic paint over the softer orange area, being careful not to cover the blue exposed in the crackling.

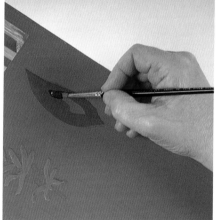

9 Lightly pencil over the traced image, as the powder will smudge away. With a small pointed brush, paint all the leaves and stems of the herbs with a mid-green paint, working flat shapes up to the outlines. For a little variety of color, add a touch of blue to the bay and rosemary, and a touch of yellow to the marigold leaves.

8 With a pencil draw up the images to the required size onto tracing paper. Position the trace images on the cupboard and secure with low tack tape, so that the image does not move around.

Then position the tracing paper underneath, graphite side down. Using a ball-point pen or a medium pencil, trace through the image onto the cupboard.

10 Paint the basic flat flowers, using orange for the marigolds, lilac for the rosemary and chive, and cobalt blue for the borage.

11 Add highlight details in yellow or white to pick out leaf veins, petals and roots, and shadow details by mixing dark blue with the "base color" to give shape to the leaves, flowers and stems. Varnish to seal and protect.

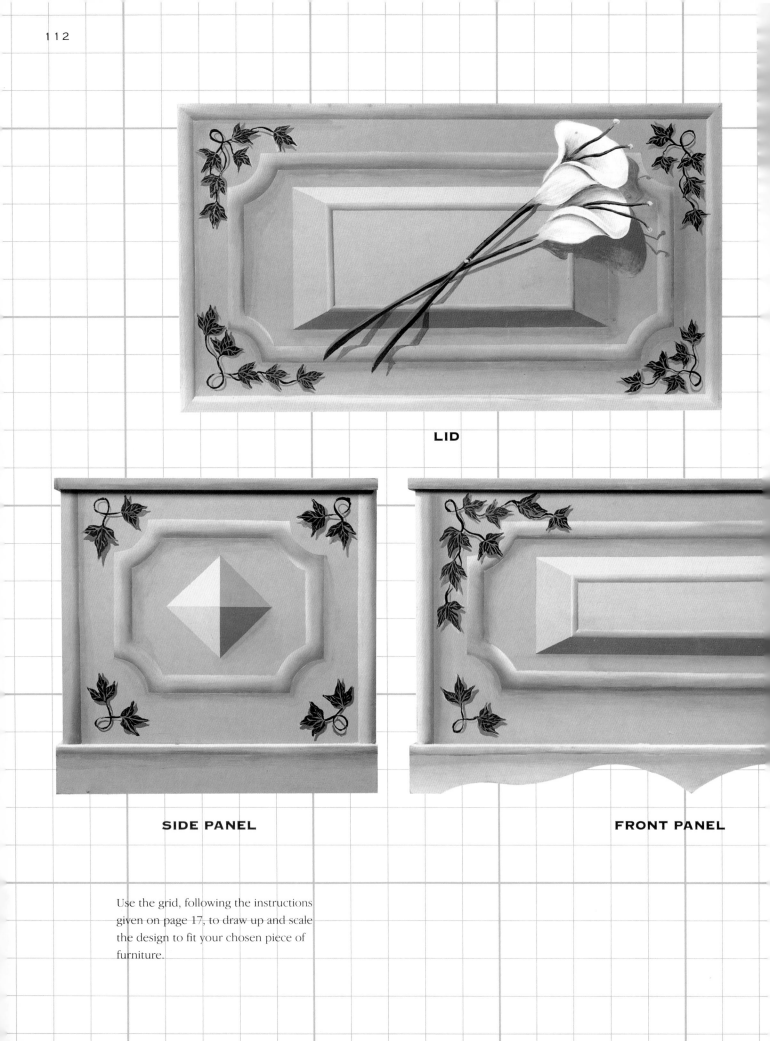

LID

SIDE PANEL

FRONT PANEL

Use the grid, following the instructions given on page 17, to draw up and scale the design to fit your chosen piece of furniture.

TROMPE L'OEIL PANELED BLANKET BOX

OLD SOLID, PANELED FURNITURE LOOKS FANTASTIC WITH THIS SIMPLE TROMPE L'OEIL EFFECT. YOU CAN ACHIEVE THAT SAME WEIGHT AND DEPTH ON A PLAIN FLAT MODERN BLANKET BOX.

YOU WILL NEED

- *2in (5cm) brush*
- *Taupe colored acrylic paint*
- *Measuring tape*
- *Compass*
- *Pencil*
- *Ruler*
- *Masking tape*
- *Craft knife*
- *White acrylic paint*
- *Raw umber artists' acrylic*
- *Black acrylic paint*
- *Three small fitches*
- *1in (2.5cm) brush*
- *Chalk*
- *Green acrylic paint*
- *Satin-finish varnish*

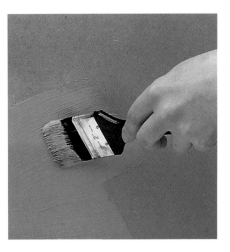

1 With a 2in (5cm) brush, apply a base coat of taupe colored paint. Apply a second coat if needed and allow to dry.

2 Measure out the paneling and beading and mark in the lines with a pencil. Use a compass for the arced corners on the beading around the central panels. Erase any unwanted lines.

In the same way, create trompe l'oeil panels on the doors of a wardrobe or cabinet.

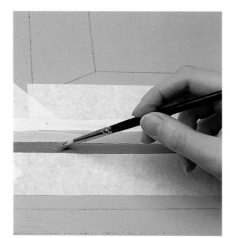

3 Mask around both sides of the beading with the arced corners. With a craft knife, carefully cut around the curved lines.

4 Pour some of the taupe color into two new containers. Mix some white acrylic paint into one and some raw umber and a touch of black into the other. Using a separate small fitch for each tone, apply equal bands of the darkest tone then the original taupe and the new lightened shade. Light the beading from the top and one side. This will mean that the lightest shade will be applied to the top of the horizontal beading and, in this case, to the left of the vertical beading.

5 While the bands of color are still wet, blend them into each other along the beading using a dry 1in (2.5cm) brush.

6 Pour some of the lightest tone into a new container and lighten it further still with white. Pour some of the darkest tone into another new container and darken it further by adding more raw umber and a touch more black. Now you will have four tones plus the original taupe. Using the same logic of lighting, apply the new lightest tone to the top left hand side of any paneling and the new darkest tone to the opposite side. Apply the other two, mid-tones to the remaining faces of the panel.

7 The front and top flat panels will be exactly the same tones as the side diamond panels with the flat, front face of the panel the same mid-light tone as the lit side. Use masking tape to keep the lines sharp.

8 Mark out a 1¾in (2cm) border around the front of the flat-topped panels on the front and top of the box. Draw a line from each outside to inside corner. Mask this mitered line and each side of the beading, and again, working in sections, apply the same process as steps No 4 and 5 (always following the same lighting logic).

9 Add a shadow to emphasize the three-dimensional effect of all the beading and paneling. To do this, apply a line of the mid-dark tone alongside the dark (shadow) side of the beading and panels.

10 While the shadow line is still wet, wash the line out into the background color using a wet 1in (2.5cm) brush.

11 Any beading which goes around a corner (i.e. around the lid and down each side) should be blended as one piece. Beading which is lit from the top will blend from light to mid to dark, and beading which starts in the shadow tone will blend through to mid to light around the edge and then back to mid through to dark again on the other side of the beading face.

12 With a stick of chalk draw groups of ivy leaves on the top, sides and front of the box.

13 Across the top of the box, sketch in two Madonna lilies with chalk. Apply flat base coats of green acrylic paint to the ivy leaves and lily stems and white acrylic to the flowers.

14 To keep the trompe l'oeil effect, highlight the lit side of the lily stems by adding white to the green paint. Also, with the darkest shadow tone used on the paneling, paint in a shadow of the lilies and the ivy leaves. Make sure the highlights and shadows on the leaves and flowers follow the same lighting logic as the paneling. Allow all the paint to dry and finish with a satin varnish to protect.

GALLERY OF DESIGNS

WITH INSPIRATION DRAWN FROM BOTH TRADITIONAL AND MODERN SOURCES, THIS SELECTION OF DESIGNS SHOWS THE ENDLESS POSSIBILITIES FOR CREATING UNIQUE AND STYLISH PIECES OF PAINTED WOODEN FURNITURE.

COUNTRY FLOWERS

The effect here is simply achieved with an acrylic wash of blue over the natural wood on the main body of the piece. The panel design is very suited to the character of this cupboard depicting a trellis and wild berries; the hand lettering gives the embroidery feel.

DESIGNER BED

Not only is there a craze for painting up old pieces but new styles are joining the world of painted wooden furniture. This stylish and unusual bed is an example of the latest in "designer" painted wooden furniture. The sections have been painted in different colors and the 50s-style motif has been applied with silver metal leaf. The inspiration for this design was starlight and night sky.

MONOCHROME

Designs which use just one color can be very effective for painted furniture, as this piece shows. The design spreads itself boldly across the drawer divisions with the flair of a William Morris wallpaper. Wallpaper and fabric paints are excellent sources of motifs for painted furniture.

CRAFT-STYLE CHAIR

Bold, bright and busy, this craft-style chair would cheer up any kitchen with its checks, stripes and spots. The back crossbars and the seat have been color washed with a strong turquoise acrylic, with a pale yellow border wash around the seat giving the piece a distressed look. The Van Gogh-style apple is a great finishing touch plonked on the middle of the seat!

RED TAG

Another interesting example of a 90s designer piece of painted wooden furniture. The smooth curved shape is the result of careful carving and the use of gesso under the bold black-and-white painted design. Gesso is traditionally made from whiting (a fine white powdered chalk) and rabbit skin glue. These are heated and mixed together to a smooth plaster-like mixture which is applied to the wood and, when dry, can be finely sanded.

VOYSEY INSPIRED SIDEBOARD

This 1905 sideboard has been carefully painted using colors and motifs of the era when the piece was originally made. The motif was copied from an original design by Charles F. Annesley Voysey (1857–1941), who was an important architect and furniture and fabric designer and a leading figure of the arts and crafts movement. The rubbed-back two-color paint finish and the blistered paint technique on the panels give the piece an aged look.

BLANKET CHEST

Boxes and chests have always been popular items of furniture to paint. The design on this blanket chest was created by using combs to make the stripes on the black diamonds and using a shaped piece of wood to make the repeat patterns on the blue and white areas. The border around the top, bottom and feet of the chest was painted white and then sponged over with a blue/gray color. This design is the result of playing around with patterns and different paint techniques.

FLORAL CLOCK

Old-fashioned motifs of beautifully painted flowers and fruits on a rich dark background give this clock a Victorian feel. The clock face has a marble paint effect, and the figures on the clock, the borders and ribbons have been painted in an antique gold paint.

MULTI-DRAWER, MULTI-COLORED CHEST

This chest has been given a loud and proud new image by using every primary color available and a different design on each drawer. Even the knobs on each drawer have been painted in a contrasting bright color to the drawer design. The finished piece has a vibrant patchwork quilt look to it.

WHITE DAISY STAINED CABINET

The use of the natural stained wood as a background to the folk art-style motif gives this bedside cabinet a rural folk feel. This approach to painted wooden furniture is a tradition that grew in the Alpine regions of Scandinavia and in the American colonies. If the piece to be painted is made from good wood with an interesting grain, utilize it as an interesting background to your design.

MULTI-COLORED CHEST OF DRAWERS

If flowers and fruits and pretty motifs are not your style then multi-colored geometric shapes, stripes and simple abstract motifs might be the answer. This type of design works very well in a plain modern setting of white walls and bare wooden floors. So, if you never go for wallpaper or busy fabrics but long for a splash of color somewhere in an interior, then a mass of bright colors confined to a piece of wooden furniture is always worth a try.

CARVER CHAIR

This designer chair has modern and classic influences in its design and shape. It has been painted in a mixture of flat, bright modern colors in some areas, and a distressed finish has been applied to some of the more classical shapes on the piece, again using strong 90s tones. The unusual arms on the chair have been given a leopard-like motif which gives their exaggerated shape a paw-like quality.

MATCHING TABLE AND CHEST OF DRAWERS

By the same artist as the floral wardrobe seen opposite, this duo of table and chest of drawers has been painted with a pale distressed background, and the floral motifs have been organized loosely, like a wallpaper or fabric design. The motif design on the chest of drawers has been painted without regard for the drawer divisions.

BIRD CABINET

This small and meticulously painted cabinet cleverly combines a leafy border with branches for detailed birds on the front panel. The background to the sides, border and top has been painted in pale woody color and then darkened around the edges with a richer woody tone. The beading around the top and bottom of the cabinet has been painted in the same rich, dark turquoise used on the panel.

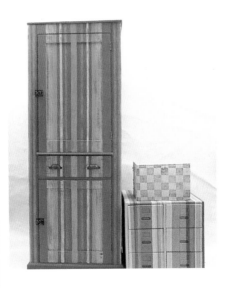

PALE CREAM FLORAL WARDROBE

This very attractive design has a clean, fresh pale but distressed background treatment on the wood, giving the piece a neutral but interesting starting point. These traditional-style motifs of flowers have been organized in a modern way, like randomly placed ceramic tiles.

STRIPED WARDROBE AND CHEST OF DRAWERS

This cheerful multi-colored striped wardrobe and chest of drawers have a fabric feel to them. Any divisions of drawers have been completely ignored and the bold stripes reign over the pieces uninterrupted by any of the item's detail, as if the furniture has been wrapped from head to toe in a piece of striped cloth.

CRAQUELURED FLORAL TABLE

This plain two-tiered table has been given more interest with a coat of bright yellow paint, a detailed floral border around the top tier and a finishing craquelured varnish. As the name suggests, craquelure is a traditional French product and is a transparent varnish which is designed to craze when drying. Some stainer is rubbed into the dry craquelured varnish to bring out all the detailed cracking, providing an interesting aged finish to the underlying artwork.

CHECKERED CABINET

This intriguing piece undeniably belongs to the twentieth century. The cabinet has three compartments on either side which have been stained and left plain, and a central inset which has a sheet of mirror glass at the back. The blue-and-yellow check design has been painted to look like ceramic tiles and produces an interesting effect with the mirror.

ORANGE FLOWER CHEST OF DRAWERS

In this design, the drawers have been treated individually, depicting an assortment of fruit and flowers on each small drawer. A combination of all the small drawer motifs has been spread across the larger bottom drawer.

MOTIF LIBRARY

THE MOTIF OUTLINES SHOWN HERE PROVIDE AN EASY WAY OF REPRODUCING SOME OF THE MORE DETAILED DESIGNS IN THIS BOOK. YOU CAN EITHER SIMPLY TRACE ROUND THEM OR COPY THEM IN ANY SIZE YOU REQUIRE.

POPPIES (see *Poppy Chest of Drawers,* page 54)

AUTUMN FRUITS AND LEAVES (see *Autumn Leaves Bookcase,* page 64)

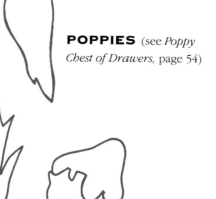

MAP OF THE WORLD
(see *Maps and Granite Table,* page 38)

CLOWN, SEAL AND ELEPHANT
(see *Circus Design Bookcase,* page 76)

ROSES AND ROSE LEAVES (see *Ribbons and Roses Headboard*, page 84)

IVY LEAVES (see *Trompe l'oeil Blanket Box*, page 112)

BUNCH OF GRAPES (see *Italian Fresco-style Cabinet*, page 90)

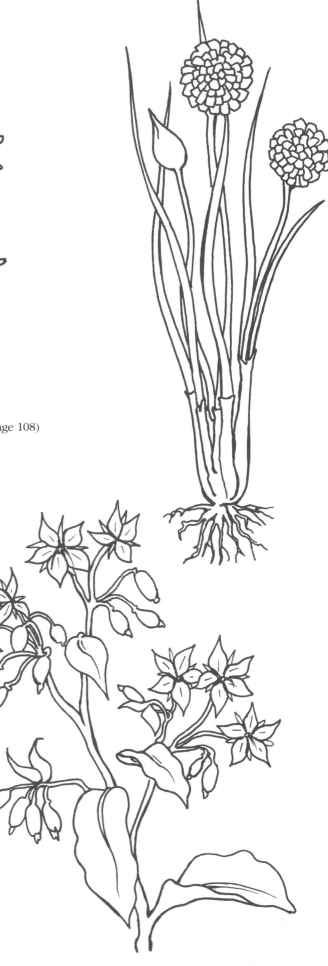

HERBS

(see *Herb Cupboard,* page 108)

INDEX

CREDITS

Quarto would like to thank all the artists who have kindly allowed us to reproduce photographs of their work in this book. They can be contacted through Quarto.

Key: T = top B = below C = center R = right L = left

Alexandra Abraham of Special Effects Decorative Arts Studio **p.118** (BL & BR), **p.121** (TL); John Eric Byers **p.121** (BL); Bette Byrd **p.119** (BC); Kate Caish **p.119** (BL); John Graham **p.120** (BC); Fabiane Garcia **p.119** (TL); John Gillah of Artifex **p.119** (TR); Kim Lowe **p.118** (TL); Katie Potter **p.121** (BR); Rare Creation **p.119** (BR), **p.120** (TR & BL), **p.121** (TL & TC); Yuko Shimazu **p.118** (TR); Judith Westguard **p.120** (BR); Lana Williams **p.120** (TL).

All other photographs are copyright of Quarto Publishing plc.

We would also like to thank the project makers: Ray Bradshaw, Pippa Howes, and Kerry Skinner, Rare Creations.

Items of furniture used in the projects were very kindly supplied by:

Ikea, 255 North Circular Road, London NW10 0JQ
(p.23, p.27, p.33, p.51, p.75, p.95)

Blankers, The Old Vicarage, Stockland, Honiton EX14 9EF
(p.67, p.71, p.107, p.117)

Harvey Baker Design, Unit 1, Rodgers Industrial Estate, Alberton TQ4 7PJ
(p.79, p.111)

Index by Dorothy Frame.

Variation artwork by Tig Sutton.